Astrology

Unlocking the Secrets of the Zodiac, Tarot, and Numerology along with Moon, Sun, and Rising Signs

Copyright 2021

The content contained within this book may not be reproduced, duplicated or transmitted without direct written permission from the author or the publisher.

Under no circumstances will any blame or legal responsibility be held against the publisher, or author, for any damages, reparation, or monetary loss due to the information contained within this book, either directly or indirectly.

Legal Notice:

This book is copyright protected. It is only for personal use. You cannot amend, distribute, sell, use, quote, or paraphrase any part, or the content within this book, without the consent of the author or publisher.

Disclaimer Notice:

Please note the information contained within this document is for educational and entertainment purposes only. All effort has been executed to present accurate, up-to-date, reliable, complete information. No warranties of any kind are declared or implied. Readers acknowledge that the author is not engaging in the rendering of legal, financial, medical, or professional advice. The content within this book has been derived from various sources. Please consult a licensed professional before attempting any techniques outlined in this book.

By reading this document, the reader agrees that under no circumstances is the author responsible for any losses, direct or indirect, that are incurred due to the use of the information contained within this document, including, but not limited to, errors, omissions, or inaccuracies.

Free limited time bonus

Stop for a moment. I have a free bonus set up for you. The problem is that we forget 90% of everything that we read after 7 days. Crazy fact, right? Here's the solution: we've created a printable, 1-page pdf summary for this book that you're reading now. All you have to do to get your free pdf summary is to go to the following website: https://livetolearn.lpages.co/silviahill/
Once you do, it will be intuitive. Enjoy, and thank you!

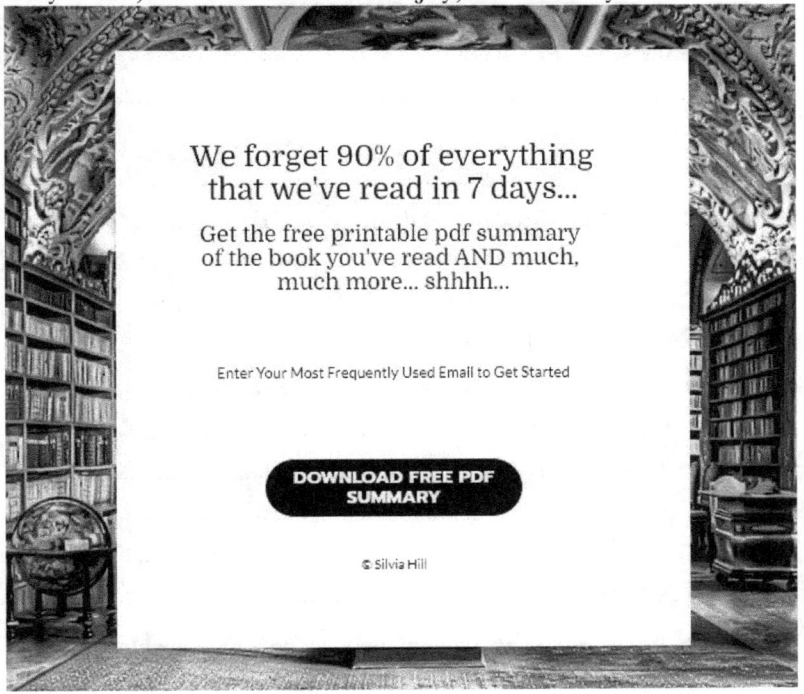

Contents

INTRODUCTION 1
PART ONE: ASTROLOGY BASICS 5
CHAPTER 1: THE PLANETS AND THE SIGNS 6
    NATAL CHARTS 7
    PLANETS 8
    ZODIAC SIGNS & PLANETS 9
    THE HOUSES 13
CHAPTER 2: THE SUN SIGN: YOUR IDENTITY 16
    WHAT IS SUN SIGN ASTROLOGY? 16
    HISTORY OF SUN SIGNS 17
    SUN SIGNS AND THEIR MEANINGS 18
    MODALITIES 23
    ELEMENTS AND POLARITIES 24
CHAPTER 3: THE RISING SIGN: YOUR MASK 26
    WHAT IS THE RISING SIGN? 26
    HISTORY OF RISING SIGNS 27
    CALCULATING YOUR RISING SIGN 28
    SYMBOL KEY 29
    RISING SIGN PERSONALITIES 29
    HOUSES OF THE BIRTH CHART 34
    EFFECTS OF YOUR RISING SIGN 35
    UNDERSTANDING YOUR RISING SIGN 35
CHAPTER 4: THE MOON SIGN: YOUR EMOTIONS 37

THE MOON 39
THE MOON AND THE SUN 40
SEEKING BALANCE 41
HOW MOON SIGNS MANIFEST 42

PART TWO: THE SECRET POWER OF NUMEROLOGY 46
CHAPTER 5: WHAT IS NUMEROLOGY? 47
HOW IT WORKS 49
WHAT IT CAN DO FOR YOU 50
THE TRAITS OF NUMBERS 51
THE MASTER NUMBERS 54

CHAPTER 6: DISCOVER YOUR DESTINY NUMBER 56
CHAPTER 7: FIND YOUR LIFE PATH NUMBER 64
LIFE PATH NUMBER 65
HOW TO FIND YOUR LIFE PATH NUMBER 65
INTERPRETATIONS OF THE LIFE PATH NUMBERS 67

CHAPTER 8: EXPLORE YOUR PERSONALITY NUMBER 74
MASTER NUMBERS 76
PERSONALITY NUMBER MEANINGS 77

CHAPTER 9: REVEAL YOUR HEART'S DESIRE NUMBER 84
FINDING YOUR HEART'S DESIRE NUMBER 85
HEART'S DESIRE NUMBER INTERPRETATIONS 86

PART THREE: HOW TAROT MEETS ASTROLOGY AND NUMEROLOGY 93
CHAPTER 10: WHAT IS TAROT? 94
CULTURAL AND HISTORICAL BACKGROUND OF TAROT 94
MAJOR ARCANA CARDS 95
MINOR ARCANA CARDS 118

CHAPTER 11: THE FIRE SIGNS AND THEIR TAROT CARDS ... 120
FIRE SIGNS 121
FIRE SIGNS AND THE SUIT OF WANDS 121

CHAPTER 12: THE EARTH SIGNS AND THEIR TAROT CARDS 129
EARTH SIGNS 129
EARTH SIGNS AND THE SUIT OF PENTACLES 130

CHAPTER 13: THE AIR SIGNS AND THEIR TAROT CARDS 138

- Air Signs 138
  - Air Signs and the Suit of Swords 139
- **CHAPTER 14: THE WATER SIGNS AND THEIR TAROT CARDS** 147
  - Water Signs 147
  - Water Signs and the Suit of Cups 148
- **CHAPTER 15: MASTER THE MINOR ARCANA WITH NUMEROLOGY** 155
  - The Four Suits of the Minor Arcana 155
  - The Minor Arcana Tarot Cards and Numerology 157
- **CHAPTER 16: UNDERSTAND THE MAJOR ARCANA WITH NUMEROLOGY** 164
  - The Story of the Major Arcana Cards 165
- **CHAPTER 17: THE MAJOR ARCANA AND THE PLANETS** 173
  - Major Arcana Cards and Corresponding Planets 174
  - Understanding the Sun, Moon, and Rising Signs 177
  - Major Arcana Correspondences of the Sun, Moon, and Rising Signs 180
- **CHAPTER 18: TAROT SPREADS** 183
  - The One-Card Spread 184
  - The Three-Card Spread 185
  - The Celtic Cross Spread 188
  - Interpreting the Cards in the Celtic Cross Spread 189
  - The Zodiac Spread 191
- **CONCLUSION** 194
- **HERE'S ANOTHER BOOK BY SILVIA HILL THAT YOU MIGHT LIKE** 199
- **FREE LIMITED TIME BONUS** 200
- **REFERENCES** 201

Introduction

Astrology and the concept of horoscopes thrive in a symbiotic relationship and alter each other's course at every step. The study of astrology and its related elements has been in existence for centuries. In fact, it can be dated back to the point when time was first measured and studied. The word "astrology" is divided into two parts - Astra, meaning "star," and Logos, meaning "reason" or "logic." The movement, position, and alignment pattern of the stars and celestial bodies are studied to interpret the vibrations and energies around us. These energies can then be utilized to manifest your dreams and understand the essence of life.

Astrology and astrological energies exist without forcing anyone to believe in them. Whether or not you believe in astrology and the energies surrounding you, their existence is not affected. However, if you take an interest and try to analyze these energies, you can benefit from them. You can learn more about your true personality and inner traits and use this knowledge to discover your inner calling and life's purpose. With time, you can also study effective ways to use your internal power and turn the tides of change in your favor.

Fundamentally, astrology combines the study of different celestial bodies, their positions, people's intuition, and a bit of science and mathematics. The study is conducted through symbols, patterns, and cycles that systematically present the findings. Since the movements of the planets are measurable, the results can be recorded, allowing us to understand the fundamental aspects of our physical realm. These movements and events trigger the cosmic waves and frequencies of the universe, which can be altered and aligned with our internal vibrations. In turn, this will cause an expected and successful outcome. It is not as easy as it sounds, though!

You must learn the right way to interpret these cosmic waves using your intuition and spiritual voice. With these things, you can discover the secrets of the world around you and use the language of astrology to interpret the singularities of the universe. One effective way to do that is to draft your horoscope or astrology chart based on the position of the celestial bodies at the time of your birth. Every person has a dedicated horoscope or a personal map and ruling planets indicated by their time and date of birth. Simply put, your astrological chart is a snapshot of the universe's position during the exact moment of your birth. This is your personal blueprint that acts as a toolkit throughout your life. You can use this toolkit to know yourself better, listen to your inner or true voice, and make desirable changes to your life.

Interestingly, every astrologer has their own way of interpreting astrological charts. While some refer to the cosmic influence and its related theories, others use the concept of space and time to perceive the Earth and heaven as one. Other domains include the study of numbers known as numerology and reading a set of illustrated cards related to one's intuition known as the Tarot. A set of root numbers is extracted in the former, based on the person's date of birth. This unique number can be used to study a person's traits, motivations, and life direction.

The essence and motto of astrology are that each person is unique and possesses an unprecedented calling. Furthermore, every person falls under one of twelve zodiac signs based on their birth month. These groups represent unique archetypes, each with its own emotional, mental, and spiritual traits. Each zodiac sign is represented by a symbol, a set of numbers, colors, and natural elements. When studying your zodiac sign and linking it to your horoscope, you can relate to your past and present, as well as foretelling your future. While the zodiac signs are stationary, you can measure your progress and future based on the position and movement of the planets. Using accurate data on the place, date, and time of your birth, you can correlate your existence to the Astral charts and one of the houses you fall under.

With the right information and practice, you can dramatically improve the quality of your life and gain emotional independence. Astrology abides by the notions of living with free will and having a strong sense of purpose, unlike those who are demotivated and fail to understand the meaning of life. It does not ask you to believe in fatalism or superstition but rather persuades you to recognize your unique skills and talents. This study helps unveil the "real" you and encourages spiritual maturation.

Since most people are unaware of the actual reasoning and fail to comprehend astronomical phenomena, they have false notions and refuse to believe the authenticity of this discipline. Now, if you are one of them, it is time to unravel the truth and legitimacy of this study, so you may become more self-aware and understand your true self. This is where this book will help you. It will enable you to examine the contrasting nature of horoscopes and astrology. Since astrology is intricately linked to our sense of being and reality, it is necessary to dispel the myths surrounding it to better understand and appreciate it. With time and practice, you can study the signs and alignment of the stars on your own and alter your perspective to achieve favorable effects.

This book contains valuable information related to astrology, numerology, the positioning of planets, sun signs, moon signs, and Tarot. It will walk you through the distinct facets of astrology and various domains in the simplest manner. Whether you are a novice or an avid practitioner, you will gain useful insights to help you on your life journey. Each chapter is broken down into fragments that can be easily absorbed. Take this opportunity as a guiding thread that will allow you to lead a more content life. Finally, this book will provide insights and tips to apply these postulates and shift your perspective to better life outcomes.

Read on to grasp the concept and philosophy behind astrology and its related entities in detail and experience its positive effects to turn your life around. Without further ado, let our exploration journey begin!

Part One: Astrology Basics

Chapter 1: The Planets and the Signs

Astrology has been a subject of fascination for centuries. Each civilization had its own notions about the stars and the planets in the sky. Many ancient civilizations developed their own unique systems of astrology. It is believed that the Mesopotamians pioneered the science and practice of astrology around 2000 BCE. The system they created greatly influenced those devised by other civilizations in the future.

The Romans, Greeks, Persians, Hindus, and Chinese all possessed knowledge in reading the planets and stars. The ancient civilizations used these readings to predict events like wars, droughts, floods, or deaths. This shows just how important and influential astrology has been throughout history and across the globe.

The classic phrase "As above, so below" is the essence of astrology. It is believed that the set of instructions written in the sky will affect worldly matters to a great extent. Since the position of the stars and the planets is ever-changing, the precise arrangement of celestial bodies at the time of a person's birth supposedly influences their destined course in life. This means that planets and zodiac signs obey the natural laws of the universe. It is these laws that all civilizations have attempted to study and codify to determine their fate.

The most common features in most astrological systems comprise planets and signs. Planets have always been considered significant in influencing a person's life events, personality, and more. Zodiac signs have existed in most cultures, with most cultures having 12 signs.

In this opening chapter, we'll set out to explore the different meanings and interpretations of terms like planets, zodiac signs, natal charts, etc. These concepts all play major roles in our lives, and understanding them helps us uncover many mysteries surrounding our destiny and desires.

Natal Charts

First things first, it's essential to understand the role and significance of the individual components we're about to discuss. Then, later in this chapter, numerous things will be covered, such as houses, planets, and zodiac signs.

Natal Charts, also known as Birth Charts, are the exact positioning of the different planets in different houses on the day you were born. These are prepared using your name, date of birth, and sometimes your place of birth. You'll find free tools available online to get your Natal Chart mapped out.

A Natal Chart will reveal a great deal about your tendencies, personality, hidden desires, and even the decisions you will take in life. This chart will be more detailed and accurate than any horoscope you may read since a Natal Chart is unique to everyone. Now, let's find out which components make up a Natal Chart.

Planets

Ten planets in astrology influence us, thanks to their unique characteristics. While planets help express various aspects of our personality, the zodiac works differently. Everyone has a different zone of comfort depending on the planets. A domicile planet is the one that rules your zodiac sign and harbors where you are most efficient.

It is important to understand that we also refer to the sun and moon as planets in astrology. This might go against the notions of human-defined modern science, but our perspective here is different. Any celestial body visible from the earth is considered a planet in the realm of astrology. What follows is a brief overview of the qualities that the different planets have. The influence that each planet has on your life will be defined by the qualities it possesses.

- **Sun:** The sun symbolizes vitality, vigor, ego, stamina, and radiant energy.
- **Moon:** The moon is a symbol of emotions and governs our moods and instincts.
- **Mercury:** The symbol of intellect and reasoning. Mercury controls how you learn.
- **Venus:** The symbol of love, attraction, and beauty. Venus determines how you attract your desires.
- **Mars:** The planet of aggression, desire, ambition, and passion. This planet determines how you act.
- **Jupiter:** This planet represents luck, optimism, and growth in life.
- **Saturn:** A symbol of discipline and hard work. This planet influences structure in life.
- **Uranus:** Freedom, sudden change, eccentricity, and rebellion are the features of this planet.

- **Neptune:** This planet represents a mystic and intuitive mind. It influences a person's artistic creativity.

- **Pluto:** This small yet powerful planet is responsible for the transformation and evolution of life.

Zodiac Signs & Planets

Think of a zodiac as an imaginary belt of the heavens through which planets move across the sky. The different stars are divided and grouped according to their shape and size into larger groups, known as constellations. Since the Sun moves through this belt once a year, we obtain a 360-degree eclipse. This eclipse, when divided into 12 equal parts, forms the components of a zodiac sign.

The zodiac signs are further grouped into four categories based on the basic constituent elements of the universe:

Elements	Zodiac Signs
Earth	Taurus, Virgo & Capricorn
Fire	Aries, Leo & Sagittarius
Water	Cancer, Scorpio & Pisces
Air	Gemini, Libra & Aquarius

The planets play a much larger role in the zodiac as each is responsible for influencing people's lives. Each planet is thought to influence the human mind in a particular manner. However, this influence varies from one individual to the next as it changes according to the different positions of the planets at different given times.

Each zodiac sign has its own domicile planet with which it is associated. A domicile planet plays an important role in determining the qualities attributed to a zodiac sign. In this section, we will explore some of how the ruling planet influences a zodiac sign.

1. Aries: Mars

As the Roman god of war, Mars perfectly matches the temperament of the first sign of the zodiac. Mars stands for ambition, passion, instinct, and aggression, and with the fiery personality of an Aries, Mars can actually bring forth its aggressive nature. Those born under the sign of Aries are adept at leadership and are known for having high energy levels. The true nature of an Aries influenced by Mars comes out when challenged or confronted in any situation.

2. Taurus: Venus

Taurus is an earth sign, meaning it has a natural affinity for earthly pleasures and materialism. While Venus is the goddess of love and beauty, the planet also symbolizes luxury and pleasure. The sensual and pleasure-seeking Taurus exemplifies the nature of Venus.

3. Gemini: Mercury

The fast-footed and sharp-tongued messenger of the gods, Mercury, is at its best when expressed in Geminis. Gemini is an air sign known for being quick-witted, chatty, and inquisitive. Geminis are usually gifted with high intellect and love to socialize. Mercury allows Geminis to think and analyze, which is something they naturally like doing.

4. Cancer: The Moon

Those born under the sign of Cancer are the most emotional of all the zodiac signs due to their being very sensitive and caring. The Moon's intuitiveness perfectly complements the nurturing nature of Cancers. They are empathetic and in touch with what everyone around them is feeling. The Moon influences our emotions, feelings, and a general sense of comfort, which is why being coupled with a gentle sign like Cancer allows these qualities to shine through.

5. Leo: The Sun

Leos like to be the center of attention at any place or event. This is why the center of our solar system is the ideal planet for this sign. A Leo's loyal, dramatic, confident, and generous nature is the perfect channel for the Sun's radiant positivity, warmth, and generous, life-giving sunlight. So, thank the Sun for your high confidence levels and positive outlook, Leos!

6. Virgo: Mercury

We know that the Roman god Mercury had multiple tasks to handle. Likewise, the planet Mercury has also been assigned to two zodiac signs. The witty and quick side of Mercury is channeled by Geminis, while Virgos channel the other side. Mercury is also a translator and interpreter, which is reflected by Virgo's keen intellect and analytical skills. As a Virgo, you love organizing your belongings, and all your plans are well prepared and executed. Be grateful to Mercury for making you so meticulous.

7. Libra: Venus

Venus is the second planet on our list to govern more than one zodiac sign. The goddess of love has a lot of love to share, after all! As the zodiac symbol of balance and harmony, the Libra seeks balance in everything in their life. The romantic and loving nature of Venus manifests itself when Libras try to maintain a happy, fulfilling love life. Libras are also artistic and have an eye for beauty, which matches Venus perfectly since the planet also represents beauty.

8. Scorpio: Pluto

A dark and mysterious sign like Scorpio was bound to be associated with the strangest of all planets. Pluto, the god of the underworld, represents the eccentricity and extreme nature of

Scorpios to perfection. The little planet has a significant impact when it comes to life-changing transformations, birth, death, creation, and destruction. Scorpio energies evolve and transform when influenced by Pluto, which makes them the perfect partners.

9. Sagittarius: Jupiter

Jupiter is the planet that symbolizes expansion, free spirit, carelessness, and optimism. Those born under the sign of Sagittarius are often happy-go-lucky people who exude positive vibes around them. The joyful planet Jupiter perfectly complements the optimism of a Sagittarius. In addition, Sagittarians have a thirst for knowledge due to the effects of Jupiter. They are also keen on trying out new things and rarely turn down new experiences.

10. Capricorn: Saturn

Saturn is the planet that deals tough love to its zodiac signs and adds some structure. As such, only a Capricorn can properly align with Saturn. Capricorns are disciplined and hardworking, which is necessary to satisfy Saturn's demand for structure. The impact of Saturn can be restrictive at times, but it also teaches Capricorns not to take shortcuts in life and always to work hard.

11. Aquarius: Uranus

Uranus is the planet that inspires rebellion, brilliant ideas, and innovation. The air sign Aquarius is the perfect match, thanks to the revolutionary energy resting inside of it. An Aquarius is naturally innovative and easily comes up with solutions that exhibit "out of the box" thinking. With the presence of Uranus, an Aquarius can have brilliant new ideas, but it is also responsible for the rebellious nature of the zodiac sign. Sudden changes, which are the signature feature of an Aquarius, shine through when Uranus interacts with the sign.

12. Pisces: Neptune

The god of the oceans is naturally suited to the mutable water sign that is Pisces. Neptune brings with it an aura of illusions and poetic beauty. The Pisceans are particularly receptive to this influence - thanks to their emotional and spiritual nature. Neptune can inspire a Piscean to be more artistic and to dream bigger. This helps turn the dreams and ambitions of a Piscean into reality.

The Houses

The houses are yet another important aspect of the science of astrology. Each house has a different set of traits that will influence your life. This depends on the location of the planets in each house at the time you were born. Astrologers often use this knowledge to predict the areas of your life in which you will experience trouble or find opportunities.

Whenever a planet visits a house, that part of your chart is influenced, and you acquire that house's traits. The first six houses are called "Personal Houses," and the last six are called "Interpersonal Houses." These houses move from self to society as we move counterclockwise.

So, let's have a look at all the different houses and discover which areas of life they have the most influence on:

- **1st House:** Also known as the house of Aries, this house is all about the beginning of things. It covers first impressions, new beginnings, your self-image, and any new initiatives you undertake.

- **2nd House:** This house governs your perception and immediate surroundings. All the things like the smells, sights, sounds, and even tastes in your life fall under this house. Led by Taurus, this house also deals with how you handle material possessions.

- **3rd House:** This house is presided by Gemini and tells us all about communication in our lives. It reveals how we interact with our siblings, parents, and society in general.

- **4th House:** This house lies at the bottom of the zodiac wheel, controlling all the foundations of life. It is home to cancer, the most sentimental sign, and it has to do with our roots and origins, which is why it determines the type of relationship a person has with their father. The parental home, childhood circumstances, and even the relationships with our family members can all be determined by this house.

- **5th House:** Leo is the ruler of this house and has imbued it with the dramatic attributes they are known for having. This house concerns all matters related to creativity in our lives and pleasure in the form of love affairs.

- **6th House:** The house ruled by Virgo commands all the aspects of one's life regarding health, wellness, organization, and discipline. Healthy and natural living and being of service to others are the fundamental traits that govern this house.

- **7th House:** Ruled by Libra, this house is all about relationships, both personal and professional. For instance, how we select our romantic partners and business partners is all determined by this house.

- **8th House:** This dark house, which the mysterious Scorpio governs, deals with all the metaphysical aspects of life and loss. Loss, which can be material loss or loss through death, falls under the purview of this house. It tells us how a person deals with the various losses they face and can even reveal how people deal with other's property.

- **9th House:** Sagittarius rules this house, and it is concerned with how we learn about spirituality in our lives. It governs philosophy and existentialism. This house is also the house of journeys to foreign lands, enriching our spiritual development as well.

- **10th House:** This house rests at the top of the zodiac wheel and is responsible for the choice of profession or career a person makes. It also governs the relationship that one will have with their mother throughout their life. This is why the 10th house, ruled by Capricorn, is the one that affects our general development in life.

- **11th House:** Aquarius rules this house, determining how we interact with our friends, teachers, and other well-wishers. This house shows us how we fit in with society and is often the determining factor in our friendships.

- **12th House:** Last, this is a house that paints the larger picture. Not surprisingly, Pisces governs this house since it deals with self-sacrifice and escapism. This final house covers all the loose ends left by the other houses, such as old age, seclusion, isolation, and much more. This house is also responsible for creativity and an interest in arts in light of its isolated nature.

These are all the basics you need to know about astrology. The basic terminologies and variables have been clarified by now. Using this information, you can easily determine what a Natal Chart represents. These are the first steps in understanding astrology, and the subject will be developed in detail in the next few chapters. So, once you have made your way to the end of this book, you will be able to appreciate the beauty and logic of astrology like never before!

Chapter 2: The Sun Sign: Your Identity

Finding yourself and understanding who you are can be quite a difficult thing to do. Essentially, you are a complex combination of emotions, ideas, values, and traits that sometimes seem contradictory. This is where your sun sign comes in. It can tell you things about yourself that you may not have recognized or even realized were a part of your personality. By interpreting your sun sign, you can get a concrete idea of who you are and learn more about your identity. If you don't know the first thing about sun signs, that's okay! Just read on to discover everything you need to understand better what they are and how they can help you figure out what kind of a person you truly are.

What Is Sun Sign Astrology?

Sun sign astrology is an iteration of Western astrology that only considers the sun's position when determining your sign. No matter which of the twelve zodiac signs, where the sun is at the time of your birth is considered your sun sign. This sun sign can determine your personality, character traits and predict events throughout your life. There are also planets, elements, modalities, and polarities associated with each sign, all working together to make up a personality map you can follow. As such, you can use your sun sign to help light your path and guide you throughout your life's journey.

History of Sun Signs

While the science of astrology dates to the 1600s, sun sign astrology as a system wasn't codified until 1930. A newspaper astrologer named R. H. Naylor coined the term for his column in the Sunday Express. When he wrote a horoscope for the recently born Princess Margaret, Queen Elizabeth II's younger sister, his popularity soared, and people began clamoring for horoscopes about themselves. This led to Naylor producing them regularly.

Shortly after this famous horoscope, Naylor predicted the crash of the R101 airship. He foretold that a British airship would be in danger in October, and on the 5th of October 1930, the R101 went down in flames over Beauvais, France. Other newspapers thus began including horoscopes and predictions of their own, and Naylor was pressed to reveal how the event was predicted. Over the next seven years, he outlined his system for others to follow.

In 1937, Naylor unveiled his completed astrology system, which he dubbed sun signs or star signs. It made predictions based on a person's date of birth, dividing the year into twelve distinct signs based on the zodiac. This allowed for twelve different horoscopes to appear in each column, giving readers a somewhat personalized overview of what their future held. The system of sun sign astrology used today has been refined over time and combined with other astrological concepts for a complete forecast of a person's personality, character traits, and likes and dislikes.

Sun Signs and Their Meanings

There are twelve sun signs within the zodiac. Each has its own associated characteristics and personalities ascribed to those born under it. While the sun's alignment upon your birth isn't the only factor in astrology, it is the most important when determining who you will be as a person. Every sun sign has a specific celestial body connected to them and a fixed, mutable, or cardinal modality (explained further below). Sun signs are grouped into four categories that correspond with the four base elements: fire, water, earth, and air. They also have either a positive or negative polarity assigned to them. The twelve zodiac sun signs are:

Aquarius

Aquarians are born between January 20 and February 18. You are associated with the element of air and the planet Uranus. Your modality is fixed, and your polarity is positive. The name Aquarius means the "Water-Bearer."

If you were born under the sign of Aquarius, you are independent by nature and refuse to conform to societal norms. You prefer to march to the beat of your own drum, and you will often seek tough challenges rather than take the safer and easier options. You don't mind being alone, but you enjoy the company of others. Aquarians are intelligent but can easily become bored when they lack stimulation. You may also have trouble expressing yourself emotionally.

Pisces

Pisceans are born between February 19 and March 20. You are associated with the element of water and the planet Neptune. Your modality is mutable, and your polarity is negative. The name Pisces means the "Fish."

If you were born under the sign of Pisces, you are a compassionate person and are selfless with others. You are a creative and intuitive individual, having wisdom far beyond your years. Because of your great capacity for empathy and emotional expression, you can be a bit too trusting. Pisceans are romantic and dislike cruelty of any kind. Music is very important to you, and you will most likely have developed a strong connection to it from an early age.

Aries

Ariens are born between March 21 and April 19. You are associated with the element of fire and the planet Mars. Your modality is cardinal, and your polarity is positive. The name Aries means the "Ram."

If you were born under the sign of Aries, you are a strong and direct person with plenty of energy. You tend to be optimistic in most situations and hold honesty as an important trait in people. Ariens are highly organized individuals, although they can also be temperamental. You work well with others, often taking on a leadership position when in a team or group. Your impulsiveness means you may find yourself in dangerous situations, but your willingness to fight for your goals will help you get through the challenges life throws at you.

Taurus

Taureans are born between April 20 and May 20. You are associated with the element of earth and the planet Venus. Your modality is fixed, and your polarity is negative. The name Taurus means the "Bull."

If you were born under the sign of Taurus, you are dependable and hardworking. You take a practical approach to life and are a loyal friend. Although you don't do well with change and can be stubborn, you are also patient and willing to remain committed to your goals. Taureans make excellent advisors and have a knack for making money. You like doing things with your hands, such as gardening and cooking, and are fond of fashion and trends.

Gemini

Geminin's are born between May 21 and June 20. You are associated with the element of air and the planet Mercury. Your modality is mutable, and your polarity is positive. The name Gemini means the "Twins."

If you were born under the sign of Gemini, you are the curious kind, often seeking answers and willing to learn new things. You are a gentle person who feels the need to express yourself emotionally. You can easily adapt to new situations, which is why you are constantly looking for interesting new hobbies and ideas. Geminians often have trouble making up their minds because they are interested in a variety of things. You like to show others affection and aren't afraid to engage with new people.

Cancer

Cancerians are born between June 21 and July 23. You are associated with the element of water and the Moon. Your modality is cardinal, and your polarity is negative. The name Cancer means the "Crab."

If you were born under the sign of Cancer, you are a very imaginative, sympathetic, and artistically inclined individual. You have no problem showing your emotions but are also prone to mood swings. You can be quite persuasive, which can be construed as manipulative, especially with those close to you. However, you enjoy being surrounded by loved ones and don't take kindly to those who try to harm or mess with them. Cancerians understand the difficulties of dealing with the outside world, so they will do their best to help others overcome their challenges and navigate through life.

Leo

Leos are born between July 24 and August 22. You are associated with the element of fire and the Sun. Your modality is fixed, and your polarity is positive. The name Leo means the "Lion."

If you were born under the sign of Leo, you are a passionate person with a generous spirit. You are creative and confident, tackling life's challenges with enthusiasm. Sometimes, your self-assuredness can come across as arrogance, yet your cheerfulness, warmth, and humor will often win people over. Leos thrive on attention, seeking validation from others through material possessions and status. You enjoy spending time with friends, having fun, and taking a break from your responsibilities every now and then.

Virgo

Virgins are born between August 23 and September 22. You are associated with the element of earth and the planet Mercury. Your modality is mutable, and your polarity is negative. The name Virgo means the "Maiden."

If you were born under the sign of Virgo, you are a practical and analytical person. You are well-organized and have defined goals in life. You may tend to get stuck on details due to your perfectionism, but this attention to detail also means you always put your best into everything you do. Virgins often close themselves off emotionally due to their shyness and fear of being hurt. You like to keep your environment clean and orderly, just like your mind.

Libra

Librans are born between September 23 and October 22. You are associated with the element of air and the planet Venus. Your modality is cardinal, and your polarity is positive. The name Libra means the "Scales."

If you were born under the sign of Libra, you are peaceful and diplomatic. You would rather solve conflicts with words than fists and are very easy to get along with. Equality and justice are important to you, so when you feel you've been wronged, you can hold grudges for a long time. Librans are sharp-minded and find inspiration all around them. You enjoy spending time with others and are good at working cooperatively. You like things in your life to be balanced, from your work and relationships to the leisure activities you engage in.

Scorpio

Scorpios are born between October 23 and November 22. You are associated with the element of water and the former planet Pluto. Your modality is fixed, and your polarity is negative. The name Scorpio means the "Scorpion."

If you were born under the sign of Scorpio, you are a brave and passionate person. You are very assertive, resourceful, and emotionally expressive. Scorpios are dedicated to the truth and facts, making it difficult for them to admit when they are wrong. You, despite dishonesty and tend to be suspicious of others that haven't proven themselves loyal and forthright. Due to your passion, you can be quick to anger, sometimes resulting in violence. Your natural leadership abilities mean others often look to you for guidance. You must keep your temper in check so they don't learn the wrong lessons from your actions.

Sagittarius

Sagittarians are born between November 23 and December 21. You are associated with the element of fire and the planet Jupiter. Your modality is mutable, and your polarity is positive. The name Sagittarius means the "Archer."

If you were born under the sign of Sagittarius, you are an idealist with a great sense of humor. You can be very generous and enjoy having the freedom to do the things you want. Sagittarians often love to travel. You are open-minded and allow yourself to learn about new cultures and philosophies without judgment. You tend to be enthusiastic and an extrovert who always speaks your mind, which can sometimes come off as disrespectful. However, your optimism means you will always try to find the best in any given situation and do what's necessary to achieve your goals.

Capricorn

Lastly, Capricorns are born between December 22 and January 19. You are associated with the element of earth and the planet Saturn. Your modality is cardinal, and your polarity is negative. The name Capricorn means the "Mountain Sea-Goat."

If you were born under the sign of Capricorn, you are a responsible and disciplined individual. You are well-mannered and treat others with respect. You are a serious person who doesn't like to waste time fooling around, meaning you can come off as strict and condescending at times. Capricorns make plans with realistic goals and don't indulge in fantasies. Because you hold yourself to such a high standard, you expect the same out of everyone else. You may seem like an unforgiving person when you hold others accountable for their mistakes, but you also greatly appreciate it when they work hard and do well. You are family-centered and traditional in many regards, which can sometimes lead to conflict with those who don't share similar values.

Modalities

In sun astrology, modalities refer to the part of a season that your sun sign falls under, each having defining characteristics shared by those born under the same modality, even if it comes during a different part of the year. There are three modalities: cardinal, fixed, and mutable. Here are the main characteristics for each one:

Cardinal

This modality comes at the start of a season. People with a cardinal modality are active, dynamic, entrepreneurial, and are a powerful force.

Fixed

This modality comes in the middle of a season. People with a fixed modality have great willpower, are inflexible, and resist change.

Mutable

This modality comes at the end of a season. People with a mutable modality are flexible, resourceful, and can adapt to almost any situation.

Elements and Polarities

The elements of air, fire, earth, and water are based on the four personality types proposed by Hippocrates, namely being sanguine, choleric, melancholic, and phlegmatic. These instill in you specific traits and characteristics depending on which element your sun sign is associated with. For example, the polarities determine whether you are more active or passive. These are the four elements and their personality types:

Air: Sanguine

This has a positive polarity. Associated traits include good communication, the ability to socialize, and developing goals and turning them into reality.

Fire: Choleric

This has a positive polarity. Associated traits include being strong-willed, assertive, and driven.

Earth: Melancholic

This has a negative polarity. Associated traits include cautiousness, practicality, and a focus on material things.

Water: Phlegmatic

This has a negative polarity. Associated traits include being empathetic, sensitive, and having strong emotions.

Ultimately, your sun sign can tell you a lot about your own self. You can use this information to help you grow as a person, learn your strengths and what weaknesses on which you must work. It can also help you figure out what will make you happy and what kind of people you will get along with best. The purpose behind understanding your sun sign is that you will be able to understand yourself better.

Chapter 3: The Rising Sign: Your Mask

Once you know your sun sign, the next important facet of your birth chart is your rising sign. It will set the tone for the rest of your chart. There may be aspects of yourself that you've only been presenting unconsciously, and your rising sign can help explain the reasons behind those parts of your personality. However, your rising sign isn't always the same as your sun sign. It can be any of the twelve zodiac signs, including your sun sign. Knowing what your rising sign is can go a long way towards helping foster a better understanding of who you are as a person.

What Is the Rising Sign?

Also known as an ascendant sign, a rising sign is an astrological sign rising on the eastern horizon when and where a specific event occurs. For you, this means which one was rising at the exact moment of your birth. It's one of the three pillars of your birth chart, along with your sun sign and your moon sign. Astrologers believe that combined, these create the foundation for your upbringing and personality. In addition, your rising sign dictates your "external" characteristics, that is, those aspects of yourself you show to other people. It's the mask you wear in public or the facade you put up to keep others from seeing what's underneath.

History of Rising Signs

Rising signs go all the way back to ancient Babylonians, who observed and recorded the specific times of the celestial phenomena of signs ascending in the sky. Then, in the 3rd century BC, Egyptians used the rising time of different clusters of stars to estimate the current time of night. The ancient Greeks later adopted this system called the rising sign, the "hour marker," or horoskopos. This is where the modern term for "horoscopes" originated.

Calculating Your Rising Sign

To calculate your rising sign, you must first know your sun sign and the precise time of your birth. You can find which rising sign is yours by referring to the chart below:

Your Sun Sign	12 AM to 2 AM	2 AM to 4 AM	4 AM to 6 AM	6 AM to 8 AM	8 AM to 10 AM	10 AM to 12 PM	12 PM to 2 PM	2 PM to 4 PM	4 PM to 6 PM	6 PM to 8 PM	8 PM to 10 PM	10 PM to 12 AM
♒	♐	♑	♒	♓	♈	♉	♊	♋	♌	♍	♎	♏
♓	♑	♒	♓	♈	♉	♊	♋	♌	♍	♎	♏	♐
♈	♒	♓	♈	♉	♊	♋	♌	♍	♎	♏	♐	♑
♉	♓	♈	♉	♊	♋	♌	♍	♎	♏	♐	♑	♒
♊	♈	♉	♊	♋	♌	♍	♎	♏	♐	♑	♒	♓
♋	♉	♊	♋	♌	♍	♎	♏	♐	♑	♒	♓	♈
♌	♊	♋	♌	♍	♎	♏	♐	♑	♒	♓	♈	♉
♍	♋	♌	♍	♎	♏	♐	♑	♒	♓	♈	♉	♊
♎	♌	♍	♎	♏	♐	♑	♒	♓	♈	♉	♊	♋
♏	♍	♎	♏	♐	♑	♒	♓	♈	♉	♊	♋	♌
♐	♎	♏	♐	♑	♒	♓	♈	♉	♊	♋	♌	♍
♑	♏	♐	♑	♒	♓	♈	♉	♊	♋	♌	♍	♎

Symbol Key

Aquarius = ♒

Pisces = ♓

Aries = ♈

Taurus = ♉

Gemini = ♊

Cancer = ♋

Leo = ♌

Virgo = ♍

Libra = ♎

Scorpio = ♏

Sagittarius = ♐

Capricorn = ♑

Rising Sign Personalities

Each rising sign has certain traits and characteristics that can determine your overall personality. They also have specific strengths and weaknesses assigned to them.

Aquarius

Strengths: You are an independent and unique person. You remain calm and collected in most situations and are tolerant of other people's views. In addition, you are sociable, using your intelligence and charitable nature to make friends.

Weaknesses: You tend to rebel against norms, even when it isn't advantageous. You often act before you think, which can get you into trouble. Due to your strong spirit, you dislike authority and taking orders.

Pisces

Strengths: You are kind and friendly to others, usually taking their feelings into account during interactions. You have an even temper, which helps you make good decisions instead of acting on emotions. You are a creative dreamer, always striving to reach the goals you set for yourself.

Weaknesses: You don't like confrontation, leading to you avoiding or running away from problems. You tend to be overly sentimental, clinging to the past. You sometimes struggle with making decisions, and your nature as a dreamer means you may have unrealistic goals and standards for yourself.

Aries

Strengths: You are adventurous, showing passion and bravery in everything you do. You can easily adapt to new situations and usually keep a cheerful and hopeful attitude in your endeavors. You are dynamic, have plenty of energy, and value honesty. You are a warm and generous person, giving to others without reservations.

Weaknesses: You can be slightly impatient and impulsive, which can cause trouble. You may be naive about the realities of certain people and situations. You are also prone to bickering, especially with those who you perceive as dishonest. Your willpower can cause issues with others, as you don't shy from getting your way with things.

Taurus

Strengths: You are a hard-working and passionate person. You can be decisive and patient, persevering against all odds. You are logical and practical and prefer to be realistic in any situation. You also have a romantic side and can be kind to others. In addition, you are very artistic, pouring your energy into creative endeavors.

Weaknesses: You can be stubborn and needy at times. You hold your values in such high esteem you may be prejudiced against those who don't share them. Your pursuit of hedonistic activities can also take you down a very selfish path. Because of your logical mind, you don't get along well with those who are fantastical dreamers.

Gemini

Strengths: You are smart and quick-witted, a warm, charming person who can get others to like you with ease. You can be very insightful have a cheerful disposition. You get along with different types of people, understand their points of view, and connect with them on many levels.

Weaknesses: You can be capricious, especially when it comes to friends. You tend to gossip, especially since you often see deeper into a person's mind than others. Your ability to charm people can also evolve into manipulation, which may cause others to perceive you in a negative light.

Cancer

Strengths: You are a kind and caring person with a gentle heart. You are dedicated and persevering, never letting obstacles stop you from achieving your goals. You have a great imagination that serves you well in creative undertakings. You also have an acute sixth sense and can perceive things about people and the world by instinct.

Weaknesses: You can be greedy at times, wanting more of the things you desire than you deserve. You are very possessive about people and material things and rarely want to share them with others. You may be a touch too sensitive, often getting your feelings hurt over the slightest offenses. You are also somewhat prudish, and you see people who are comfortable expressing themselves with a skeptical eye.

Leo

Strengths: Like the lion of your sign, you are a proud individual. You show unwavering loyalty to those you consider friends or family, having their back through thick and thin. You are charitable, giving to others without a second thought, and are enthusiastic in all your endeavors. You also can reflect on things, garnering a better understanding of any situation.

Weaknesses: Your pride can quickly turn into arrogance if you're not careful. You may behave conceitedly, believing you are above others. You tend to be somewhat wasteful, especially when you've got what you needed from something. Your willfulness can also land you in trouble since you refuse to back down.

Virgo

Strengths: You are highly intelligent and use your powerful mind to your advantage. You strive for perfection in everything you do, holding yourself to very high standards. You are precise in your actions and prefer to be practical. Your sense of style is elegant, and you enjoy the finer things in life. You are also very perceptive, picking up on subtle hints and social cues that others often miss.

Weaknesses: Your perceptiveness can sometimes lead to you becoming nosey, getting involved in other people's affairs when they may not want you to do so. Your preciseness and elegance may come across as fussiness. Also, your perfectionist nature can become overbearing, making excessive demands of others.

Libra

Strengths: You are an idealist, always seeing the best in people and situations. You are very reasonable and show a willingness to compromise. You are charming, have excellent social skills, and can deal with many personalities without trouble. You are kind and fair-minded and always want to see justice done. As an artistic being, you enjoy things like music, painting, and various crafts.

Weaknesses: You have a penchant for laziness and procrastination. Because of how easy socializing comes to you, you may be careless, especially when it comes to other people's feelings. You are prone to egotistically behaving since you are often the center of attention. You don't like to commit to things and prefer to live a free-spirited life.

Scorpio

Strengths: You are an intelligent and rational person. You have great intuition and are insightful, discovering things about others that people often overlook. You are independent and don't rely on others for your own happiness. You are devoted to those you care about and are very reasonable, acting in a manner that benefits everyone in difficult situations.

Weaknesses: You tend to obsess over things until it becomes unhealthy. You are often suspicious of other people's motives, partly because you can perceive aspects of them they may be trying to hide. You can be arrogant and complicated at times. As a possessive person, you don't want to let anyone else have what you hold close to your heart.

Sagittarius

Strengths: You are outspoken about your views and aren't afraid to stand up for yourself. You have an upbeat personality, lifting the spirits of others when they're down. You are brave and adventurous, never afraid to take on a new challenge. You always look on the bright side and manage to stay optimistic even in the face of uncertainty. You are also rational, using your mind to solve problems as efficiently as possible.

Weaknesses: You can be forgetful, constantly losing things like your keys or failing to remember important dates and events. This can seem like being thoughtless, as when you forget someone's birthday or overlook their contributions, it may come across as malicious. You are also somewhat rash, letting your outspokenness take over, which doesn't always lead to positive results.

Capricorn

Strengths: You are a very dependable and reliable person. You are intelligent, and there is something endearing about you, helping you make many friends. You can be persistent, pushing forward even when you face setbacks, and are determined to persevere no matter what. You are generous to others and have an unfailing optimism. You prefer practicality in things, such as buying a plain vehicle that gets great gas mileage over a flashy sports car that burns through fuel.

Weaknesses: You are a solitary person who would rather do things on your own. While this isn't always a bad thing, you avoid asking others for help, even though you're the first to offer it. You can be stubborn, refusing to admit you're in the wrong, or do things someone else's way. You may be suspicious of others, and you question their honesty during everyday interactions.

Houses of the Birth Chart

Birth charts are divided into individual "houses" that correspond to the twelve signs of the zodiac. It involves a complex system that charts the zodiac signs based on the movement of the Earth as it rotates on its axis. The first six houses are considered to be below the horizon, whereas the other six are above the horizon. They possess specific traits assigned to them, and all have a name that expresses their overarching meaning. These houses are:

1. Aries: Life: House of Self
2. Taurus: Gain: House of Value
3. Gemini: Sisters: House of Sharing
4. Cancer: Parent: House of Home and Family
5. Leo: Children: House of Pleasure
6. Virgo: Health: House of Health
7. Libra: Spouse: House of Balance
8. Scorpio: Death: House of Transformation
9. Sagittarius: Passage: House of Purpose
10. Capricorn: Kingdom: House of Enterprise
11. Aquarius: Good Deeds: House of Blessings

12. Pisces: Rehabilitation: House of Sacrifice

Effects of Your Rising Sign

Various factors can determine the potency of a force in your birth chart. Most astrologists believe that the closer to the start of a given sign a person's birth falls under, the more strength it will possess. This is because most of the first house will be within that sign. When their birth comes later in the sign, the majority of the first house falls into the next sign, causing it to be weaker. When the sun is in a weaker position, like at the bottom of your birth chart, the rising sign is believed to have more influence, this is because the sun would have been on the other side of the Earth at the time you were born.

The influence of your rising sign may weaken at the age of 29, at which point you will become more like your sun sign. This is due to people becoming more confident as they get older, meaning there's less reason to wear a mask in public. However, this isn't true for everyone, as there are still plenty of people who put on a facade their entire lives. With more self-esteem and a better-developed ego, you can express your true inner self without fear. Ultimately, you can use your understanding of your rising sign to help you grow and become a stronger individual.

Understanding Your Rising Sign

Once you understand your rising sign, you gain deeper insights into how you behave around other people. You'll know the strengths you can take advantage of and offset your weaknesses. Knowledge of your rising sign can help you adjust your attitudes and tendencies, allowing you to connect with others on a deeper and more genuine level.

It's worth remembering that your rising sign is only but a part of your identity. Your actions and decisions are still up to you, but knowing and understanding your rising sign can inform these actions and decisions to help you make better ones. The sun, moon, and stars aren't responsible for how you interact with other people; they merely provide guidance to assist you in your development and growth as a person.

Chapter 4: The Moon Sign: Your Emotions

When it comes to exploring behavioral tendencies and character traits in astrology, most people only refer to the star or sun sign. Many people fail to realize that the sun, the moon, Mercury, Venus, Mars, Jupiter, Saturn, Uranus, Pluto, and their rising sign are all significant celestial bodies in the realm of astrology. Each planet, along with the sun and the moon, symbolizes a different set of characteristics and qualities in us humans. Each rules over a certain aspect of our lives, contributing its energy and direction. Every celestial body is a character of its own. They all have their unique interests, goals, and functions. Based on the zodiac sign they are positioned in, they express themselves and act independently.

We constantly feed off the energy of the sun, the moon, and the planets. However, how they affect us typically depends on their position in the zodiac at any given moment. As we've seen, who you are is a collection of your natal planets at the time of your birth. You may consult an astrologer or look for an online birth chart calculator to know your natal planets. Once you discover where the celestial bodies lie in your natal chart, you can tell how they impact different parts of your life and affect your energy. You can also explore the relationships between the planets.

Now, to better understand how your natal chart determines who you are as a person, you must first understand the role and functions of each celestial body. As explained previously, the sun sign reflects yourself and your conscious mind. It determines your life's purpose and fosters your creative energy. In simple terms, it is the most solid and genuine version of who you are.

The sun naturally rules over Leo. Mercury is the planet of expression, communication, intellect, and reason. It represents your ability to carry out coherent and reasonable conversations.

Mercury naturally rules over Virgo and Gemini. Venus rules over Taurus and Libra and is the planet of love, romance, pleasure, and beauty. It symbolizes how you construe value, love, and experience luxury and pleasure. Mars represents your desire and sexual drive. It determines raw energy and aggression, namely your fundamental physical instinct.

Mars rules over Aries. Jupiter is the planet that pushes you to chase your loftiest dreams. It's associated with good luck, optimism, and abundance and naturally rules over Sagittarius. Saturn is renowned as the rigid celestial body. While its energy can be harsh, it is intended to help you learn and grow.

Saturn is associated with discipline and life lessons and naturally rules over Capricorn. Uranus is perhaps the most unpredictable planet. Its energy is innovative and original, and it represents awakenings, inspiration, and insights. Uranus naturally rules over Aquarius.

Neptune is the planet of sensitivity and spirituality. It is the most ethereal planet, representing intuition, artistic expression, and dreams. It rules over Pisces. Although it is no longer considered a planet in science, Pluto is still as much of a powerful planet as any other planet in astrology. Pluto represents transformations, death, darkness, and rebirth. It has an intense energy that symbolizes extremities, from the newest beginnings to all endings. Pluto was even named after the god of the underworld and rules over Scorpio.

Finally, the moon. Throughout this chapter, we will explore how the moon plays a central role in the zodiac world. The moon, which naturally rules over Cancer, can be thought of as your internal emotional compass. It is a gentle and emotionally driven celestial body.

The Moon

In astrology, the moon symbolizes those aspects of yourself that you can't express. It represents your innermost emotions and rules over your most vulnerable and hidden parts. The moon holds the key to what makes us feel comfortable, safe, and emotionally secure. It regulates all the aspects of yourself that you don't show to others unless your emotional and safety needs are met. The moon is often called the cosmic mother. Just like it represents our emotions, it symbolizes our motherly, feminine, and maternal side. It also represents our memories and even the simplest things we find joy in. It is also a representation of our inner child. In other words, the moon reflects our basic, natural reactions, profound personal needs, and our unconscious.

Our moon signs are a reaction to our suns' activities. It has a reflective power, receptive energy, and responsive reactions. The moon is spontaneous and ultimately instinctual. The role of the moon in the solar system mirrors its purpose in the zodiac. The moon's circular motion around the sun can be viewed as a symbol of protectiveness, just like how it teaches us, or rather, wants us to protect ourselves.

The moon grants us our liveliness and spirit. It controls the rhythmic rise and fall of our energy and activity. It is the arbitrator between the exterior world and the inner world. It is irrational, unlike the sun. Everything, including our habits, prejudices, spontaneous thoughts, reactions, and feelings, is ruled by the moon. The sun censors most of it, which is why these feelings may not be acted out.

The Moon and the Sun

For some people, the moon drives and affects their personality much more than the sun does. This holds true, especially if your moon falls in a water sign, namely Scorpio, Cancer, or Pisces. Your moon can also be predominant in your personality if your moon is at a conjunct angle in your natal chart. This means it can be near a 4th or 10th house cusp, a Descendant, or an Ascendant. To attain happiness in your life, it's best to give your moon neither too little nor too much attention. Remember it without obsessively analyzing your actions or emotions accordingly. Grant Lewi, an Astrologist, offered the most accurate description of the moon. He explained that when you feel something that you can't quite explain, it's because your moon is aware of it, but your sun refuses to say it. He claimed that the things you feel too deeply (things you can't even cry out) are the thoughts that emerge from the nature of your moon.

Silent sorrows, clandestine dreams, indescribable ecstasy, and the cryptic version of yourself that no one seems to know, value, or understand all originate in your zodiac's moon. When you feel misunderstood, it indicates that the nature of your moon is not in line with the sun's energy. Sometimes, most of us experience the frustration of knowing what needs to be done but not knowing the right way to do it. This typically happens when your moon and your sun fall out of tune. It's the moon that's aware, but it's the sun that refuses to cooperate. When you question your actions or words, it is because either your sun or your moon acted despite the other. Most of the time, if you find yourself satisfied with your unexpected speech or action, it's the moon that acted against the sun's will. By contrast, if you find yourself bothered or critical of yourself, it's the other way around.

Seeking Balance

Once you've analyzed your natal chart and understood the energies of your sun and moon, you can figure out a way to maintain a balance in your life. If, as it happens, your sign and moon fall under the same sign, this suggests that the things you want and the things you need are in alignment. When you think of your path in life and your ability to express yourself cohesively and freely, it's because you may feel less resistance in doing so typically.

If your sun and moon are downright incompatible, you may be prone to internal stress and tension. This is because the two celestial bodies are constantly trying to find a way to satisfy each other's needs along with their own. Our emotional needs differ from our conscious ones. For instance, if your sun is in Virgo and your moon is in Gemini, you may find yourself constantly fighting a battle between seeking practicality and wanting variety. You may have to overcome several obstacles before finally finding true happiness and balance. You can set yourself out on the path to self-discovery once you understand and accept the differences between your sun and your moon. This is needed so you can unite and please both aspects of who you are.

The sun and moon always work together, whether to maintain life in the universe or within your inner self. However, just like they've found harmony in existence, it is your role to help them achieve harmony within you. This doesn't necessarily mean that you should attempt to make your moon and sun seek the same things, which is impossible. It simply means you should look for the good in what each offers. Besides, their inherent polarity is what allows you to grow and progress. As they work together, despite their differences, they allow you to move on and let go of the things that hold you back and hinder your progress. At the end of the day, your sun and your moon want you to thrive in their unique ways.

How Moon Signs Manifest

Like sun signs, moon signs manifest themselves differently. Moon signs have different emotional needs, express themselves differently, and have different reactions. Unlike the sun, the moon moves quickly around the zodiac. The moon stays in the same sign for a two-day period. This is why you need the date, time, and place of birth to calculate your moon sign accurately.

Emotional Aries

If your moon is in Aries, you may be very short-tempered. You probably like competition and challenges and feed off any form of excitement. You find satisfaction in releasing built-up energy, and while this is good, it may severely hurt the other person even when it no longer affects you. However, one of the best things about emotional Aries is that they don't hold grudges. Once you talk about your emotions, you are quick to move on, forgive and forget.

Emotional Taurus

You feel safe only when you are provided with stability. It's almost impossible to satisfy this need with the constant unpredictability of life. As a result, you tend to be practical, relying on the material aspects of the world. You will easily get hurt if you don't accept that change is inevitable.

Emotional Gemini

Gemini moons tend to run away from their emotions by unintentionally playing vicious mind games. Once their emotions are challenged, they find a way to view things exactly as they want, rather than how they ought to be. However, Gemini moons are intelligent and curious. They have a fun nature, and when they allow their feelings to surface, they can be open and sentimental.

Emotional Cancer

If you are an emotional Cancer, you feed off your feelings. Even when things seem logically solid, you rarely contradict your emotions. Most of your decisions are made based on instinct. You may get hurt easily, though you still have a protective layer that will instinctively come into play to safeguard itself. You are somewhat tactical and resilient and are emotionally strong. You can easily walk out on people and never look back once they run out of warnings or second chances. When treated well, though, you are a very nurturing, loyal, and warm individual.

Emotional Leo

You find security in your ability to impress others. Receiving admiration and praise is your drive and makes you feel safe. However, when you find yourself the center of attention, you can feel confused. You naturally desire success, money, and eminence and can attain it all.

Emotional Virgo

Your security rests on clarity and structure, even when it comes to your emotions. You may feel a strong urge to get everything in order. This can cause you severe damage and hinder your mind, which is why you must accept that things are typically imperfect. It's simply the nature of life.

Emotional Libra

If your moon is Libra, you probably seek safety in your relationships. In addition, you wish to be a source of happiness to others and favor an abundant and rewarding social life. In the end, though, focus on yourself more and figure out the things that satisfy you. As an emotional libra, you have a strong desire for a harmonious and balanced life.

Emotional Scorpio

With your moon in Scorpio, you may feel the need to go as deep in your emotions as possible. Normally, delving this far into your feelings can cause you to feel vulnerable. While exploring and understanding your emotions is a good thing, it also means you can never let go of anything that hurt you. This also makes it difficult for you to do anything that you aren't willing to do.

Emotional Sagittarius

As someone with a moon in Sagittarius, you are always searching for something. This is your ultimate desire. You find safety in adventure and exploration. You like intriguing beliefs and philosophies. You are always searching for things, missions or goals, to give your life meaning. You choose to experience the higher vibrations of life, allowing you to let go of negative emotions rather quickly.

Emotional Capricorn

You get your safety from feeling useful. You want to benefit those surrounding you. You want to help society and seek explanations from the external world. Unfortunately, your need for validation can cause you to feel unloved and useless, leading you to overlook your own needs. You must trust your potential instead of worrying about others ignoring you.

Emotional Aquarius

If you're an emotional Aquarius, chances are you have a complex relationship with your emotions. You feel the need to liberate yourself from negative emotions. You want to free yourself from anger, jealousy, fear, and other unwanted feelings. While this may temporarily grant you peace of mind, this will build a lot of pressure and bottle up your emotions in time. Besides, when others show negative emotions, they will expect you always to tolerate them.

Emotional Pisces

Those with Pisces moon are characterized by their discernment and sensitivity, which may leave them feeling insecure at times. Motional Pisces are usually passive when it comes to their future and life in general. They will simply sit back and watch things as they unfold. However, if you are into spirituality and creativity, you can unlock boundless chambers of imagination.

When it comes to the world of zodiacs, people mostly direct their attention to their sun or star signs. However, what they don't know is that the positioning of their moon matters just as much. Your moon is everything that your sun represses. It's the unconscious and your hidden, unspoken emotions. Exploring your moon can be your key to unleashing your creativity and your path to self-discovery.

Part Two: The Secret Power of Numerology

Chapter 5: What Is Numerology?

Whether we're talking about our everyday life or in spiritual terms, not surprisingly, numbers hold significant value. Throughout this chapter, we explore the significance of numbers in the spiritual world. Numerology, simply put, is the correspondence between a number and its spiritual nature on individuals and the concept of existence as a whole. Keep in mind that numerology can also refer solely to the study of the alphabet's numerical value.

For centuries, people have experimented with different ideas and concepts in numerology. However, it wasn't until 1907 that the word numerology itself was scripted in the English language. Babylon, ancient Egypt, China, Japan, Rome, and Greece were among the earliest civilizations where the first records of numerology emerged. Pythagoras, the Greek Philosopher, is historically known as "the father of numerology." He was highly celebrated for being an incredible mathematician and scholar. Although much of Pythagoras' life is a mystery, his interest in numbers is well-recognized in history. Driven by his passion, he traveled to Egypt, where he spent 22 years studying Chaldean numerology. He believed that the power of numbers is the essence of all existence and that the entire world was built upon it. According to Pythagoras, everything in life can be translated into a numerical form. This led to developing the Pythagorean number system, which is still applied in modern technology. This system is based on the idea that letters can be assigned numerical values.

Numbers also have a major significance in religion. For instance, some say that the number 888 represents Jesus, the Holy Trinity's infinite nature, and Hanukkah, which lasts for eight nights. The number 666, on the other hand, is linked to the beast. In Tarot, every card has a number with a unique and distinct meaning, and in the Chinese tradition, bad luck is highly associated with the number 4. Thus, numerology is important in every aspect of our lives. We subconsciously use it to find meaning in different things. Some people even unintentionally master the art of numerology to employ it in the stock market! But most combine numerology and astrology to set themselves on the path to clairvoyance and self-discovery.

Let's point out that numerology is not to be confused with astrology. While they are very different studies, they both aim to discover individuals' unique qualities, characteristics, and traits. Astrology and numerology rest upon distinct concepts and ideas. However, they can be and typically are, used together in various ways. For example, people combine the two fields to make predictions and attempt to understand themselves and others. Numerology and astrology both use mathematics, science, and spirituality to decipher readings for the future. In fact, Prem Jyotish, a numerology and astrology expert, offers one of the clearest explanations as to how numerology can be used to that end. He explains that numerology employs significant numbers in your life (numbers that revolve around it) as signs that can allow you to find different things that can help you without being tied to a specific timeline or schedule.

On the day you are born, the planets, the sun, and the moon align to create your energy. Their positions in your zodiac continue to affect you as they move. Understanding their position in relation to your zodiac can help you get a better sense of your behavior, emotions, reactions, and ultimately, who you are as a person. Meanwhile, by combining the letters of your birth name with their respective numbers, numerology can help you gather insight into your future. This will reflect your personality traits, motives, challenges, talents, and karma energy. Astrology and numerology are both needed to leverage the readings you gather from both studies. Your astrological inferences can be faulty if not based on divisional charts and an accurate interpretation of them. This applies to numerology as well. How freely you express your emotions and blend with the environment that surrounds you can both affect your numerology readings.

How It Works

The science of numerology can be very esoteric. If you are looking for accurate and highly detailed readings, you may need to resort to a certified numerologist. However, simple calculations such as those for your personality, expression, life path, and soul's urge numbers can be easily obtained. Connecting the dots and figuring out how all of these numbers come into play together is why you need an expert. Invariably, numerology predictions can provide profound insights into different aspects of life. They can also help you learn more about other people. The most basic readings and calculations can reveal incredible revelations. Like the infinite nature of numbers, a numerology chart can be read and interpreted in endless ways.

What It Can Do for You

Besides providing the keys for predictions and self-discovery, numerology, when used correctly, can help you discover the hidden meanings of existence. Think of numerology as your own personal guide to life. It dictates your possibilities, potential, strengths, and weaknesses. The three numbers derived from your name (the personality, power, and soul's urge numbers), along with the other three derived from your birthdate (life path, attitude, and birth numbers), each have their own meaning and purpose. Some say that the most prominent of them all is your life path number. Specific energies are tied to designated numbers. For example, the number "1" is associated with innovation, leadership, and independence, while the number "3" is linked to self-expression, allure, and optimism. Number 6 reflects harmony and responsibility and 9 of healing, compassion, and perfection.

While it can be confusing at first glance, understanding the concept behind the calculation is quite simple. For starters, the cosmos of your life is affected by your birth date. It determines your life's path and provides an interpretation of the relationships you cultivate. You can think of it as a beneficial insight into the unknown, a way to prepare for what's ahead. Numerology can help you tap into your potential and abilities and teach you how to make your character shine through. This is intended to help you change your own life by choosing the path you want to walk down. Many people refer to numerology when looking to make difficult or life-altering decisions. It gives them a clear insight into whether it's a suitable time to embark on new life journeys. When you set out to explore the unknown, numerology typically sends you signs to warn you about both positive and negative incomings.

Numerology can help you find your spirit's purpose and guide you towards the paths along which you can form meaningful professional and personal relationships. It gives you a clear insight into the person who will walk you through life. Numerology can also help drive you towards opportunities by letting you know the avenues that promise auspicious results. Not only that, but it also enables you to understand the mindsets, ambitions, drives, desires, and inhibitions of important people in your life. For instance, it can help you understand why some people succeed and others fail even though they work towards the same goal (wealth, status, happiness, enlightenment).

You can use numerology to discover more about your traits, set goals, and establish plans to help you attain them. It helps you make the right choices regarding education, work, finances, love, and marriage. It also allows you to find surefire ways to overcome your challenges. By using numerology to assess the energies of your environment, you will always be in the right place at the right time.

The Traits of Numbers

Have you ever wondered why numbers are divided into odd and even? This is because they share similar traits. However, odd numbers and even numbers have their own strengths and weaknesses.

Odd Numbers

Odd numbers epitomize the spirit of adventure, creativity, and inspiration. They are symbols of intangible things linked to the brain's right hemisphere. Odd numbers like to do things differently. They go against the grain, which is perhaps why they are called "odd" numbers. Let's further dig into these symbolisms:

The number 1 symbolizes the urge to drive forward and initiate. The sun and intellection are both associated with it. The number 1 is considered masculine. As visionaries and leaders, the number 1s are pioneering, direct, and groundbreaking. Their weakness, though, is that they may be too dominant and bossy. They can be overly aggressive and poor listeners.

The number 3 symbolizes the urge for artistry, self-expression, and creativity. Number 3s are thought to be gifted and naturally talented. They are lucky and optimistic, have a heightened sense of imagination and a great sense of humor. That said, number 3s are not all blessings. They tend to gossip and be unorganized. They are lost and don't have a strong sense of direction. They talk a lot, but they never act on their words.

The number 5 represents the yearning to experience every aspect of life. This longing manifests itself in mundane emotions such as the love of adventure, curiosity, and change. Naturally, the number 5 tends to be peculiar. It is also the number of boundlessness. Number 5s choose to explore and expand in all directions at all times. However, as "odd" as it may sound, number 5 may be deemed fearful. They are also usually moody, unhappy, and can even be thought of as escape artists.

The numbers 1 through 6, in both odd and even groups, represent mundane, everyday concerns. By contrast, the numbers 7 and beyond deal with higher transcendental matters.

The number 7 symbolizes the need for knowledge and wisdom and seeks to understand the realm of technicalities. The number 7s are skeptics and hermits. They like to research, observe, and investigate. On the other hand, number 7s can seem sarcastic and cynical. They are quite analytical, which is why they may sometimes appear withdrawn and depressed.

The number 9 is representative of the desire to find acceptance and amicable love. It is also associated with appreciation and compassion. The number 9 tends to be forgiving and tolerant, although they may seem bitter and moody. Number 9s are also possessive and prone to depression. Because it's the greatest odd number, 9 embodies the idea of completion. As we'll see, it is similar to the number 6 but a much wiser and grown version of it.

Even Numbers

Even numbers are tied to the brain's left hemisphere. They symbolize structured and laid-out things. As opposed to odd numbers, even numbers represent tangible things and like to conform to the norms. They don't like the unexpected and prefer that their lives go very smoothly. Generally, even numbers are associated with the "right" things in society.

The number 2 embodies tranquility, harmony, and unity. Number 2s are typically gentle and soothing. Their patience and sensitivity also characterize them. The number 2 is thought to be feminine and representative of the moon. It expresses abstract energies, feelings, intuitions, and vibrations that are hard to put into words. But number 2s can be perceived as timid. They are self-critical, overly consumed by details, and are usually reluctant to advocate for what they believe in.

The number 4 symbolizes the need for orderliness. It is structured, systematic, and seeks practicality and efficiency. Number 4s are considered down-to-Earth. The downside of the number 4 is that they can be closed off, stringent, and very opinionated. They may also lack imagination.

The number 6 feels the need to provide service. It is also symbolic of tenderness, care, and romantic love. It represents the benevolence of individuals who are very loving toward other people. This makes them patriotic, family-oriented, and devoted to others and their welfare. Unfortunately, this also makes them self-sacrificing and somehow over-protective. They can be nagging and resentful, often to unhealthy extremes.

The number 8 embodies the spirit of the law. It is majorly associated with the law of retribution. Number 8 goes by the statement, "for every action, there is an equal and opposite reaction." Number 8s are concerned with causes and effects and the concept of karma. They are structured, authoritative, and driven by the need for balance and the commandments of Jesus and Moses.

Number 8s are potent and directed, although they can be obsessive and overly driven. The number 8 is typically compulsive and miserly. However, the number 8 mysteriously stands out from the rest. It holds high energies and power.

The number zero, or the cipher, is symbolic of the fulfillment of possibilities. Zero can elevate and draw out whichever number it accompanies. It doesn't change the number's value, however. It only makes it more mature and grown. It is a way to show that the other numbers have experienced an entire cycle and are now ready to operate from higher perspectives. The cipher is an emblem of the whole world.

The Master Numbers

As the master numbers, 11, 22, 33, 44 are phenomenally special. They convey a strong sense of dedication to help with the substantial awakening of consciousness. When a master number shows up in a numerology chart, this suggests that maturity and wisdom are needed to deal with various responsibilities and life choices successfully. Master numbers comprise two single digits, and these digits can result in greater things than single digits can achieve on their own. You can know the single digit that any master number can be reduced to. For instance, the number 11 can be reduced to 2 (1+1=2), and 22 can be reduced to 4 (2+2=4). Similarly, 33 is 6, and 44 is 8.

The master number 11 encompasses the qualities of numbers 1 and 2. Eleven can also be written as 11/2. It symbolizes the force that lights up the path towards a higher sense of consciousness. Great inner flexibility and strength are required to go down that path. On the downside, 11 can be perceived as high-strung and anxious. It is easily disenchanted and contradictory. Some go as far as to say that it holds "schizophrenic" traits. It constantly swings back and forth between personalities. The need for balance drives 11/2.

The master number 22 displays the qualities of numbers 2 and 4 and can be written as 22/4. It symbolizes the need to reconstruct the world in accordance with the laws of human dignity and equal participation. However, 22/4s may indulge in self-destructive behaviors. They may be considered very negative, lazy, and even cruel.

The master number 33, written as 33/6, includes all the qualities of numbers 3 and 6. It is driven by the desire to lighten up and vitalize the world by offering humor and laughter. However, this number may feel burdened and aimless. It is viewed as a people-pleaser.

Last, the master number 44 (or 44/8) embodies the qualities of the numbers 4 and 8. It symbolizes the need for reconciliation and bridging the gap between god and goddess by employing inner spirituality and aligning the mind and body. On a mundane, social, and personal level, it is concerned with healing children. It is easily overwhelmed which challenges and the burdens of life. Ironically, 44 may seem oppressive and heartless.

Ultimately, the study and practice of numerology can help us understand the essence of existence, ourselves, and others. It offers great insights into the future, aiding us in making major life decisions. By using numerology, you can guide yourself down positive paths and find ways to overcome challenges.

Chapter 6: Discover Your Destiny Number

Numerology uses a person's Destiny Number to determine their goals in life and how those goals are to be pursued. This number, also known as the Expression Number, is easy to calculate and can help you garner meaningful insights into your true nature. However, remember that this number does not tell who you are right now but rather indicates the kind of person you could be if you fulfill your duties and follow your instincts.

The most commonly suggested way to calculate your Destiny Number is by adding up the individual digits corresponding to the letters of your birth name. While many people suggest using your nickname, others think that the only proper way to calculate it is by using the name given to you by your parents on your birth certificate. However, you can try it with variations of your name to obtain interesting results that might give you hidden insights. Of course, you should also avoid including any prefixes or suffixes like Jr, Sr, or 1st, and even the changes made to your name later in life should be avoided.

The chart used to discover the Destiny Number is rather simple and can easily be found online. It goes as follows:

1	2	3	4	5	6	7	8	9
A	B	C	D	E	F	G	H	I
J	K	L	M	N	O	P	Q	R
S	T	U	V	W	X	Y	Z	

Let's take a random name and discover the Destiny Number for it by utilizing the table. For example, if a person is named Jack Black, then the steps to discover their Destiny Number by using the values in the table will be:

1. JACK = 1+1+3+2 = 7

2. BLACK = 2+3+1+3+2 = 11 (add both individual numbers, so 1+1) = 2

3. **Destiny Number** = 7+2 = 9

After discovering the Destiny Number, you have only to match the resulting number with the given description for each number. We will later discuss how Destiny Numbers affect every individual's path in life in detail to help you better understand what your life's goals should be aligned with. These are basic guidelines to give you an overview and might include more points as applicable.

So, let's take a look at the number you calculated for your name:

Number 1

As a number 1 Destiny Number holder, you strive to be the best, and your path lies in leading others. You have a strong drive for leadership and attaining power which makes you a naturally adept leader. The unyielding determination, perseverance, and courage you exhibit inspire others to follow you. You have a strong sense of initiative and don't wait for anyone else to take the first step.

You are free of self-doubt, which is a characteristic that should not be exhibited by you when following your destiny. Your self-confidence and boldness against insurmountable odds make you a born leader. You crave independence and don't want to be stuck in a rat race like the others. This is why you'll often dive into decisions headfirst without thinking about the consequences.

With such a strong drive for success and the ability to innovate, you would excel at starting a business of your own. Your determination and the creative solutions you come up with are likely to bring great financial gains in your life. But sometimes, you might need to be gentle and more considerate towards others. Your Destiny Number will inherently drive you towards self-centeredness and egotism since your leadership approach is ruthless and aggressive. However, understand that things can be accomplished even without resorting to such extremes.

Number 2

Being a number 2, your job is to be a harbinger of peace, harmony, love, and cooperation. For you, the purpose of everything in life is to maintain love and harmony. As a result, you thrive in environments free of conflicts, and you'll always strive to appease any situation where tensions run deep.

You can excel at diplomacy and people skills if you devote the time to groom yourself properly. For you, a larger cause can be the motivation that pushes you to greatness. Even though you might not get credit for what you did, you will still be content with your contribution since your ideas matter more to you than money or wealth. However, you might be more of a dreamer than a doer, and you'll often have a hard time being practical and realizing that some things are out of reach.

You can be shy, but socializing is an essential activity for you since a lack of it would make you depressed and pessimistic. Working on your shyness, indecisiveness, and oversensitivity will enable you to cultivate great interpersonal skills. You will be admired and liked by everyone around you, thanks to your capacity to understand and empathize.

Number 3

As a holder of the number 3 destiny, you will be the life of every party or conversation around you. Being optimistic, inspiring, enthusiastic, and friendly is in your nature and will help you attract others towards you. You will easily impress people with your charms, and people will love to make conversation with thanks to your remarkable social skills.

You can develop yourself along creative lines like writing, speaking, singing, or any other performance arts. Even your destiny will align with proper devotion, so you get maximum opportunities to be on stage. For you, life is a journey that's meant to be enjoyed, and your optimism will increase as you mature. However, you must follow your passions and don't let go of what your heart truly desires, or else you may fall into a cycle of anger, depression, and self-destructive behavior.

With your ability to inspire and influence others, you'll be able to do well in a career like sales. Your only weaknesses might be superficiality and attempting to please everyone. Suppose you can overcome these obstacles and develop your personality to be positive, uplifting the spirits of others. In that case, you will fulfill your destiny of being an inspiration to those around you.

Number 4

As a wielder of the number 4 destiny, you will be naturally bestowed with the tenets of hard work and responsibility. You thrive in order and stability and will often go as far as sacrificing your own comforts to establishing and maintaining a well-functioning system. Number 4 makes for an excellent partner, whether in business or marriage, due to their unyielding devotion to a cause.

You will be happy in planning, organizing, and executing a strategy, which makes you an ideal candidate for managerial positions. You serve as a bedrock to many institutions around you, be it your family or your community. People trust you because of your demonstrated dedication and pragmatism.

You must learn to take risks if you wish to maximize your potential. You might think that if you fail, then people will think less of you, but this is only an irrational fear you must overcome sooner or later. If you pursue qualities like impeccable morals, honesty, loyalty, and seriousness, you will be the happiest since it will bring you a step closer to your destiny.

Number 5

If there's one word that can be associated with a number 5 destiny, it's freedom. You are a free soul who doesn't like to be bound by anything. You get frustrated whenever your life gets mundane or stagnates. While many others might want stability, you enjoy the sense of adventure and change. You want to explore the world and live life to the fullest.

A sedentary life is your worst nightmare, and you don't want to be stuck in a rut. For you, traveling is as much about the journey as it is about the destination. You might border into the self-centered category, and your relationships might not last a long time either. This is because you get bored of repetition and routine, even in relationships.

However, you are also a versatile person with multiple talents. You have a curious mind that allows you to be more spiritually aware and conscious than others. If you can overcome your weaknesses like fearfulness, selfishness, and myopia, then you can endorse the role that your destiny will drive you to.

Number 6

Anyone with a destiny number 6 is blessed with the ability to love, support, and nurture those in their life. You will not distinguish between friends, family, or society while sending out your love. The only thing you will care about is treating everyone with kindness and compassion.

A number 6 will find happiness in lifting the mood and raise the spirit of other people who might feel depressed. As long as you are dependable, friendly, and open to others, you will have no issues when it comes to meeting your destined goals. Those with this destiny number are often prone to overly empathizing with everyone, and they go out of their way to help out the ones in need. Unfortunately, this can sometimes work against them as they get too invested in others and overlook their own needs.

A number 6 might have many other talents, but they will most likely devote themselves to helping the poor, hungry, old, and needy. Work involving charity of any kind will be the most appealing to you due to your inherent compassion and love for others. The family life of a number 6 will be prosperous and full of love, but the negative traits you might exhibit are dominance and self-righteousness. If a number 6 can eliminate any vestiges of these negative behaviors and accept others with an open heart, then they can fulfill the role chosen for them by their destiny.

Number 7

If your destiny number is 7, you are a lifelong learner and a teacher. The purpose of your existence is to obtain knowledge and share it with others. Due to your desire for knowledge, you will most likely have a contemplative nature and find yourself poring over religion, spirituality, philosophy, and yourself.

You are a gentle soul at heart, but since your wisdom extends beyond what others might comprehend, your words may hurt others who are not aware of your intentions. You might feel the need to spend most of your time alone, but this will harm you. If you don't share your knowledge with others by interacting with them, this will lead to unforeseen frustration and depression.

Your destiny will most likely lead you towards a career of similar nature with your thirst for knowledge. You will do well as a scientist, teacher, or spiritual guru since you naturally want to share your knowledge and enlighten others.

Your only downsides are skepticism, cynicism, and superficiality. However, if you can overcome these vices, then you will fulfill your true potential and destiny.

Number 8

People blessed with the number 8 have a naturally high drive for success in the material world, and they seek to command respect and power from others. A number 8 is not an easy destiny to live up to, but if you master what is demanded of you, this number becomes one of the most rewarding ones.

A number 8 has immense potential for financial success. You will make a great businessman, and your administrative prowess will be unparalleled if you exercise proper judgment. The number 8 will have authority issues at times, making them feel like they exercise authority wherever they go. This is one of those problems that come with great power and skill. Once you overcome these basic personality issues, you will achieve a lot in the material world.

You might also face issues like stubbornness and over-ambition, but these can easily be turned to your advantage by acknowledging and addressing them. For example, stubbornness can be turned into strong self-belief and confidence in whatever you pursue, whereas your ambition can help you be more driven to achieve the true path laid down by your destiny.

Number 9

Last, a number 9 likes to be around people and interact with them with compassion and care. If this is your destiny number, you will be happiest when collaborating with others and helping them reach their full potential. You will most likely be a romantic at heart and see everything through your prism of romanticism, but when people don't measure up to your expectations, you can get disappointed.

People often see you as a mentor and expect you to guide them on their own journey since your life seems well sorted out. Friendships and other relationships are vital for your journey, as you cannot function without meaningful connections with others. You can heal and repair broken-spirited people with your charismatic and unconditional support, which helps you grow as a person.

If you don't cultivate your personality in line with your destiny, you will end up the exact opposite of what you were meant to be. For example, you can turn out to be emotionless, cold, and arrogant if you don't invest time in others since this is the only way for you to accomplish your destiny fully.

Now, after you discover your destiny number and the path laid out for you, it is your duty to follow through. There is no guarantee that you'll turn out exactly as described in the above points if you don't invest in yourself. You must work actively to sideline the negative aspects of your personality, or else they might become dominant over time. If this happens, then you can never unleash the potential of your destiny.

You can also try to find the destiny number for your nicknames to see if they paint a similar picture. Often, when you get the different destiny numbers, you can identify a mix of different qualities from both the numbers into your personality. This will help you better understand the different facets of your personality, and in turn, you will be able to follow the course of your destiny in a much more comprehensive way.

Chapter 7: Find Your Life Path Number

Numerology is the study of the relationship between numbers and the physical world. As we've seen, it is based on the teachings of the Ancient Greek philosopher Pythagoras, also known as the father of mathematics. According to Pythagoras, all things in the physical world contain the energetic vibrations of numbers. Apart from providing quantitative, real-world solutions, he believed that numbers are interconnected. Repeating numbers and numerical synchronicity have been observed for thousands of years. Numerology is a great tool for identifying patterns and making sense of recurring numbers in your life. The study and practice of numerology can help you better understand the world around you and your character traits by observing numerical patterns in your daily life.

Pythagoras and his contemporaries believed that since mathematical concepts are easy to regulate and classify, they could easily be connected with reality. Today, numerology practitioners believe that everything in this world has a numerical representation, and it is up to humans to understand the divine relationship between numbers and the events that occur throughout their lifetime. Modern numerology provides a comprehensive system to identify the main number influences found through people's names and dates of birth. Pythagoras devised a method that attributes a numerical value to alphabets. Based on his theories, the practice of numerology can help you better understand yourself.

Life Path Number

Your life path number can help you gain insight into your skills, habits, tendencies, and possible obstructions you might have to face in life. With the mystical power of numerology, and more importantly, through your life path number, you can focus on your strengths, understand and accept your weaknesses, realize your ambitions, hone your natural talents, and accomplish your life's purpose. With the help of your life path number, you can identify why certain events occurred in your past, why you are going through a certain phase in your life, or why you feel like you are running around in circles. The life path number is a meaningful tool to appreciate what you have, push your boundaries, and create a better future with the understanding of your life's greater purpose.

How to Find Your Life Path Number

To discover your life path number, you have only to solve a simple equation. According to numerology, by reducing your date of birth to a single digit, you will find your life path number. To do so, you must take the individual digits in the date, month, and year of your birth date and add them separately. You will get three different numbers. Now, add those three numbers. If it is a double-digit number, add the individual digits of that double-digit number again until you reach a single-digit number. If you got a single-digit number, that is your life path number!

Still confused? Let us take an example to find your magical life path number. How about we take some help from the renowned wizard, Harry Potter? Harry was born on the 31st of July 1980.

We'll consider the day, month, and year separately to find Harry's life path number. Let's start with the day. Since he was born on the 31st, we'll add 3 and 1, giving us 4. Since July is the 7th month of the year, we get 7 as our second number. Suppose he was born in December, which is the 12th month. We would add 1 with 2 and get 3 as our second number. Now, consider the year 1980. We add 1, 9, and 8 and get 18 as a result (a double-digit number). So, we add 1 with 8 from the number 18 and get 9 as our third number. To sum it up, we have the numbers 4, 7, and 9 corresponding to the day, month, and year of Harry's birth date. Last, we'll add the three numbers until we reach a single-digit number. So, adding 4, 7, and 9 together gives us 20. Adding 2 with 0 means that 2 is the final number and Harry's life path number.

Equation

Step 1:

31/07/1980 = (3+1) + (7) + (1+9+8+0)

Step 2:

31/07/1980 = (4)+(7)+(20) = (4)+(7)+(2+0)

Step 3:

31/07/1980 = (4)+(7)+(2) = 20 = (2+0) = 2

Life Path Number = 2

By reducing Harry's date of birth to a single digit, we've found his life path number to be 2. However, there's a catch. If, during the calculations, you end up with a number like 11 or 22, you can't reduce them further. The reason behind it is that 11 and 22 are known to be "Master Numbers," according to numerology. People who have any of these two numbers as their root number are considered special. Maybe Albus Dumbledore was one of them. Who knows?

Numerology experts believe that the formula mentioned above for calculating life path numbers is important to follow. However, they also believe that the science behind numerology has an integrated nature and a brilliant architecture of its own. Therefore, blindly adding numbers will not do you any good. Instead, you might get confused with the outcome.

Now, what are you supposed to do with your life path number? What's the meaning of all this? The explanation is simple. Each number is believed to have a specific vibration associated with different traits, skills, and challenges. Using our previous example, Harry Potter's life path number reveals that he is caring, deeply kind, and empathetic. You certainly can't deny that! To discover what your life path number reveals about your life, read on. But, before you proceed, there are a few things you should know. First, you must follow the correct procedure to calculate your life path number. Second, each life path number is associated with certain strengths and challenges. You must understand and accept your life path number to have a positive impact on your life. When you align with your life's path, you will feel more energized, motivated, and on track. Without further ado, let's move on to the meat of this chapter!

Interpretations of the Life Path Numbers

Life Path Number 1

Traits:

Self-evidently, number 1 always comes first. This number is associated with autonomy, independence, individuality, and leadership. People with the number 1 as their life path number are known to be ambitious, bold and strong, and are naturally inclined to stick to their goals. They are born leaders who usually find success in their professions. Also known to be creative and dedicated, the Ones can sometimes be bossy and big-headed. Giving orders instead of taking them is a trait found in these individuals. But generally, they are quite charming and diplomatic. The Ones are usually interesting people to be around.

Challenges

The biggest challenge people with life path number 1 face is developing a greater sense of self-confidence. They can put a lot of importance on the desires, needs, and opinions of other people. They may find themselves too busy pleasing others instead of living the life they desire. Developing a voice of their own can be a big challenge for them. They can often be overprotective and have a dominant personality which can lead to disputes with other people. They may also be prone to loneliness or anger issues. However, with practice and focus, the Ones can overcome these challenges easily. They must remember that even the most independent ones need the love and support of their friends and family.

Life Path Number 2

Traits

The Twos are known to be balance-loving people who value partnerships and love. They are deeply caring, kind, and empathetic. Known to be diplomats, people with life path number 2 are skilled at diffusing tense situations. Their diplomatic nature may also make them good politicians. Their emotional sensitivity makes them harmonious, helping them bring together opposing forces through kindness, compassion, and empathy. The Twos can easily assume the role of a mediator and tune into their heart's desires with ease. Preaching the good and leading an honest life is a known trait of the number 2.

Challenges

The deep emotional sensitivity can make it difficult for people with life path number 2 to stand up for their needs. They can find it hard to tap into that sensitivity and use it to connect with others. Their inclination to avert conflict can make them overly dependent in their personal and professional relationships. Also, their tendency to focus on the negatives may make them feel hopeless and defeated in the face of criticism or difficulties. This fear can stop them from realizing their true potential, making them feel undervalued and under-appreciated. They must adopt a positing mindset and avoid seeking external validation. They can overcome the challenges of life path number 2 by realizing that the much-needed equilibrium already exists within them.

Life Path Number 3

Traits

The number 3 represents creativity and socializing. People with life path number 3 tend to be optimistic and fun to be around. They love communicating and being in the spotlight. Their cheerful nature can keep them highly motivated and energetic. They can accomplish great things if the fire of positivity within them is stroked. They represent self-expression and are gifted with prodigious creative skills. Be it art, oration, or writing, the Threes are destined to share innovative concepts that motivate, inspire, and uplifts others. People with life path number 3 find tremendous joy in making other people happy. Known to be avid socializers, they are great at interacting with people, networking, and even romance. In short, they are a total social magnet.

Challenges

People with the number 3 as their life path number may find it challenging to remain optimistic and realistic during tough times. They may also find it difficult to commit or focus on a project they take up. More often than not, they tend to abandon their tasks and withdraw entirely. They may become too bothered by what others think of them. However, the Threes can easily mitigate their escapist tendencies by practicing peaceful mindfulness to rekindle their jubilant energy.

Life Path Number 4
Traits

The number 4 represents discipline, health, and structure. Those with the number 4 as their life path number are reliable individuals who adhere to principles and values. These traits make them desirable co-workers and valuable friends. They are blessed with earthly energy and have fortified roots that let them fulfill the expectations others have for them. They are known to be hardworking, practical, and responsible. The Fours believe in creating sound logical patterns, systems, or infrastructure that can support growth.

Challenges

These individuals are susceptible to rigidity and may become too fixated on rules and regulations. They may find themselves irritated by people who don't follow orders or break the rules. They may also find it challenging to balance their ambitions with their need for stability. By learning to go easy on the rules and norms, the Fours can feel liberated by finding the courage to take risks.

Life Path Number 5
Traits

The number 5 resonates with adventure and inquisitiveness. The Fives are intellectual and love movement and change. They make great educators and journalists, owing to their strong communication skills. They are often blessed with free-spiritedness and a childlike sense of curiosity and wonder. They can find pleasure in the simplest of things. Their love for freedom and movement compels them to experience the world in the best possible way. They tend to learn the lessons of life through impulsive yet brave acts. People with the number 5 as their life path number are known to be impulsive, playful, and vivacious.

Challenges

The Fives can easily feel bound, impatient, and restless due to their natural urge to discover new things. They may find it challenging to accept their interpersonal commitments and professional responsibilities. To overcome these challenges, people with life path number 5 must remember that the greatest discoveries and adventures lie in their backyard. They just need to narrow their gaze.

Life Path Number 6

Traits

The number 6 symbolizes family and responsibilities. Known to be natural healers, people with life path number 6 tend to be compassionate, empathetic, nurturing, and supportive. Their problem-solving skills, whether emotional or physical, make them great therapists. Their caring nature, gentle approach, and strong sense of responsibility allow them to easily communicate with friends and family, especially children or pets. The best part is that they display tenderness in whatever they do!

Challenges

The protective energy from the number 6 can make it challenging to remain consistent. That energy can quickly become controlling and dominating. To avoid over-protective tendencies, the Sixes must become understanding and build trust with others.

Life Path Number 7

Traits

The number 7 is associated with imagination, introspection, and investigation. People with the number 7 as their life path number have great analytical skills, detail-oriented, and keen eyes. Their mind makes them inventive and quick-witted. Known to thrive in the inner world, the Sevens are blessed with the wisdom and creativity that enables them to rarely get bored and entertain themselves endlessly!

Challenges

The Sevens may find it challenging to listen to their rational and logical side as much as their intuition and creativity. Their attention to detail makes them perfectionists, which is often disappointing because they quickly find flaws in any system. To keep things fun, the Sevens must counter their inner skepticism with a rational mind.

Life Path Number 8

Traits

The vibrations of the number 8 are associated with success, money, and authority. The Eights are blessed with authority and material wealth. They have the fire of ambition burning within them. They are known to be hardworking and good with money, naturally making them financially successful. Self-sufficiency and comfort are very important for this number. Their goal-oriented nature, broad thinking, and the will to race to the top can help them easily assume leadership roles and reach extraordinary success.

Challenges

People with life path number 8 can find it difficult to decide when to take charge and when to delegate. Their skill with money can also make them prone to tricksters and hustlers. However, this type's authoritative nature often makes them ignorant of constructive criticism. They must learn to pay heed to genuine advice.

Life Path Number 9

Traits

The number 9 represents acceptance, compassion, and understanding. The Nines value principles and are unwilling to compromise for convenience. They can be generous, idealistic, and stylish. Also known to be "Old Souls," the Nines are naturally spiritually aware who can help others achieve awareness. They are not afraid to transform and can transcend the physical realm.

Challenges

Life path number 9 presents a risk of codependency in personal relationships. The Nines tend to focus on the future most of all. They may have trouble anchoring themselves to the reality of the present. In other words, they must strive to balance dreams and reality.

Master Number 11

Life Path Number 11 can be understood as an amplified version of life path number 2. It is believed that number 11 is connected with spiritual awareness, enlightenment, and philosophical talents. Often, people with this life path number find their gifts under extreme circumstances.

Master Number 22

Also known as the "Master Builder," the number 22 revs up the energy of the number 4. By combining the believable with the unbelievable, Master Number 22 can cultivate dynamic platforms and create a long-term legacy—the power of Number 22 fuels intuitive and innovative thoughts that assist them all along with their transformation.

Chapter 8: Explore Your Personality Number

Your personality number is one of the most important numbers found in numerology. It forms a core part of the science of numerology, which helps you recognize how others perceive you and how your personality impacts those around you. These insights can shape your actions and plans to get the maximum benefits in your career, love life, business, or any other endeavor.

A personality number is an important tool since a personality is not an objective thing to point out. Even if you ask your closest friends, family members, or co-workers, you will get vastly different responses each time. This can make it difficult for you to understand the true nature of your personality, which you only show a minor part of two different people. However, by knowing your personality number and its associated traits, you can hope to pinpoint those qualities you would like to cultivate or the flaws you want to eliminate from your personality.

Let's consider how you can calculate your own personality number in just a few simple steps and work on the perception others have of you. First, write down your full name on a piece of paper since we need the consonants in your name to find your personality number. After that, you'll need a reference to the chart attached below (available online for free). Then, write down the corresponding number for each consonant in your name.

1	2	3	4	5	6	7	8	9
	B	C	D		F	G	H	
J	K	L	M	N		P	Q	R
S	T		V	W	X	Y	Z	

Let's assume a fictional name like JANE DOE. To discover the personality number for this name, we'll look at the table above and write down the digits corresponding to each consonant in the name.

J	A	N	E	D	O	E
1	-	5	-	4	-	-

Now, we simply add all of these digits to arrive at a single one, which in our case would be:

1+5+4 = 10 (double-digit so 1 + 0) = 1

Now that we know Jane Doe's personality number is 1, all we have to do is refer to the description for each number's personality type, given further below.

However, before we do that, there's one persistent issue that plagues the minds of anyone who's new to numerology and does not have a clue about master numbers or how to deal with the letter "Y." It's actually rather simple once you get the hang of it, so let's find out what all this fuss is about.

What about "Y"?

The letter Y is a special one as it is neither a consonant nor a vowel. That is why, depending on the situation, it can be treated as either a vowel or a consonant! Here are the two rules you need to follow to determine if the Y in your name should be counted as a consonant:

- Y as a Hard Consonant: Here, the Y will be considered a consonant if used in your name in place of a consonant. Some examples of this would be Toyota, Yuri, Yasmine, etc.

- Y Doesn't Sound Like a Vowel and Is Placed Near One: When the Y does not make a vowel sound and is placed near a vowel, it will be treated as a consonant. Some examples of this would be Grayson, Murray, Murphy, etc.

Master Numbers

Simply put, master numbers are special numbers with bonuses attached to the personality of those who possess them. The master numbers are 11, 22, and 33. You might be wondering about 44 or even 55, but the only numbers included in the triangle of enlightenment are 1, 2, and 3, which is why the other number combinations are not considered master numbers.

Master numbers are very rare, and consider yourself lucky if you have one of them as your personality number. However, these numbers abound with the traits present in their sums and even in their respective individual digits. This means that if your master number is 22, you will have the qualities of numbers 22, 2, and 4 simultaneously.

Personality Number Meanings

Every personality number has its own associated meanings and can help you gain useful insights into your personality. This section will look at the different numbers and what they might denote in your personality if you match any of these personality numbers.

Number 1

The Ones are aural leaders who are full of confidence and creativity. They have a knack for management, leading others, and coming up with creative solutions. They are determined, and this combined with their fearlessness, enables them to achieve anything they set their sights on.

The problem with Ones, however, is that they are also dominating and egoistic. They drive people away due to such heavy personalities that many get intimidated by. As a result, Ones can get overconfident, which can cause their downfall combined with their innate stubbornness.

Ones are not very compassionate, but they make up for it with a strong sense of loyalty. They are independent individuals who believe in taking a stand for any cause or issue they believe is worth fighting for.

The Ones can grow into exceptional leaders if they keep their arrogance and ego in check. This will lead to more people trusting and following them. The Ones will successfully lead their followers, thanks to the high standards they set for themselves.

Number 2

Number Twos are perhaps one of the most attractive personality types. They are very easy to talk to, honest yet gentle, approachable, and trustworthy people. Twos make very good friends, and their qualities make others trust them and confide in them.

One of the signature traits of the Twos is their peacekeeping attitude. They do not enjoy conflict and pacify any situation that might escalate. Their gentle and diplomatic nature ensures that they can tell people about anything they did wrong without hurting their feelings.

The Twos like to keep their feelings to themselves, so they are shy and sometimes get moody. They will put up a ferocious fight if they have to, despite their peaceful nature. The Twos can also turn cynical and pessimistic if under a lot of stress.

Overall, Twos are good at maintaining relationships and excel at keeping the romance alive. In addition, the philosophical and creative nature of Twos makes them instantly admired by other people.

Number 3

While Threes are naturally inclined to be extroverts, they are pretty good at interacting with others. Those with number three are highly intuitive with people-to-people interactions and observing their surroundings.

Number threes are adept at making conversation and attracting people towards them using their silver tongue. Threes just know when it's the right time to strike a conversation and are very opportunistic in that regard. They are highly ambitious and succeed at what they set out to do. Number threes are usually quite attractive to the opposite sex and are often blessed with extraordinary beauty or charm.

Threes sometimes come across as manipulative even with no such intentions, and you have to be careful about it. This is because they tend to be more biased towards the materialistic side of things and must control this nature to come across as a more well-rounded personality.

Number 4

Number Fours are a different breed altogether. With their gentle, caring, and pragmatic approach towards others, the Fours make for great companions and guides. Fours are very mature from a young age, and they are also dependable individuals. This makes them suited for leading a healthy family life. It doesn't hurt that they are family-oriented themselves.

The Fours seek stability and will choose a stable and dull life over adventure and freedom every time. The people with personality number 4 are very devoted to what they do, giving it a hundred percent in all aspects of their lives.

However, this stability-seeking and mature outlook on life makes them appear dull and boring. Sometimes, the Fours get too serious and have a hard time taking things lightly. This also reflects in their clothing, which is usually not flashy at all. Instead, they like wearing functional clothes, and their fashion sense is very subtle.

Number 5

Number Fives believe in living life to the fullest, and to live up to this standard, they have a deep love for traveling. Their adventurous side is only trumped by their high spirits, which can be contagious to others around them. Fives make great conversationalists as their spirit of adventure, combined with their philosophical mindset, gives them a considerable edge.

Fives don't stress out if anything doesn't go their way. They overcome obstacles easily and maintain their high spirits while doing so. The greatest quality Fives possess is their adaptability and versatility. No matter what life throws at them, they find a way to handle it in the best manner.

Fives are very lively and like indulging in the things that make life worth living. But if they go overboard, they can easily become addicted to food, drugs, alcohol, sex, or other dangerous temptations. Fives are also prone to burdening themselves more than they can handle, which they must avoid at all costs.

Number 6

The Sixes have very well-balanced personalities. They are compassionate, nurturing, and self-sacrificing. A number six will never go out of their way to hurt anyone's sentiments and are always available to help out anyone in need.

They are known for keeping secrets, which is why people seek them out to lighten their burden. The Sixes often sacrifice their own dreams, hopes, and luxuries to help their loved ones fulfill theirs.

Sixes never judge people hastily. They can see the inner beauty of the people because they are so beautiful on the inside themselves. However, a number Six can easily be hurt if someone says or does something reckless. A number Six who turns cynical will often become unkind and cold to others. This is why they need to keep their guards up.

Number Sixes also worries unnecessarily about money, and keeping their spending habits in check is bound to help them tremendously.

Number 7

The number Sevens are very knowledgeable people with a unique outlook on life. For them, the pursuit of knowledge is what matters most. Therefore, they are scholars who conduct themselves with grace and dignity.

The Sevens don't let other people's opinions affect them and have conditioned themselves to avoid harsh criticisms. Number Sevens are very intelligent and mysterious since they like keeping to themselves. This is the reason why they make great poets and writers. They don't care whether people like what they write since they don't do it for appreciation.

The Sevens are by no means shy or underconfident. On the contrary, they prefer solace rather than waste their time not thinking about the greater problems in life. They may often appear reserved and emotionless, which is why they must try to interact with others.

Number 8

Eights are a very successful breed thanks to their self-control, confidence, judgment, and instinct. Number Eights are best suited to positions of power and actively seek positions where they'll be able to lead and exert influence.

Number Eights strive to build their wealth and fame. They mostly become successful in these endeavors. However, their family life suffers due to this. The number Eights can be dominating and not give credit where it's due since they believe that they are instrumental in all of their successes.

That said, the Eights attract many influential and powerful people willing to help them out due to the charisma and confidence they exert. On the other hand, the Eights can be a bit headstrong and love to brag about their wealth. If an Eight can overcome these issues, then their personality can be a much more positive one.

Number 9

Nines are a happy mix of adventure, confidence, wisdom, and attraction. There is something about them that can't be identified but is extremely attractive. The Nines don't lack charisma or elegance and are adored by almost everyone they meet.

However, Nines don't become friends with people they meet right away. They might also come across as aloof or arrogant if they don't actively ensure they don't. The confidence runs high in Nines, but it doesn't for it to turn into overconfidence.

The Nines appreciate arts and the finer things in life. They are kind and spiritual and have premature intelligence, so many people approach them for advice. The Nines must keep themselves grounded, and everyone will easily like them.

Number 11

Number Elevens are very gentle personalities who like to maintain peace wherever they are. However, while they are equally strong, they might have a tough time showing it. Strife and conflict can have a very negative impact on the wellness of the Elevens, which is why it should be avoided at all costs.

The Elevens are very compassionate and care about the wellbeing of others as much as their own. They can come across as shy and are underestimated, but Elevens will not hesitate to shine through with their courage and fortitude when given the opportunity.

Elevens are also spiritual and know how to keep their composure. They are sometimes vulnerable to backlash from people who might see them as weak targets, but Elevens easily prove them wrong when they must.

Number 22

Number 22s want to bring change in the world, mostly for bettering everyone around them. They are compassionate and reliable leaders who keep finding new ways to influence the world for the better.

They are consistent, responsible, and dedicated to their work, making those around them satisfied since the 22s leave no stone unturned when assigned a task. They are also powerful leaders fueled by motivating their followers.

Sometimes, they might get engulfed in self-doubt, which is one of their biggest weaknesses. 22s might grow insecure about their abilities, but they must believe in themselves and understand that their dedication and personal ethics are surpassed by none.

Number 33

The 33s are nurturing personalities who like to take care of those around them. They are often seen as parental figures owing to their helpful, gentle nature. They are also very artistic and inspiring. Hence many people erect them as their role models.

However, the 33s can unnecessarily worry about anything and are also vulnerable to criticism or harsh comments. They are not very good at judging other people's character and sometimes feel betrayed by somebody they deeply cared for.

The 33s tend to involve themselves in the lives of others to improve it for the better. However, this quality can lead them to be taken advantage of due to their gullible nature.

These were brief descriptions of each personality type so you better understand how to mold your personality to avoid common pitfalls. Every person is unique, so there might be points that do not apply to you or some points we missed. Educating you about how to identify common perceptions about you is accomplished with these general points almost universally applicable.

Chapter 9: Reveal Your Heart's Desire Number

While the numbers associated with your personality work to reveal the perception others might have of you or the goal you should pursue in life, the heart's desire number, also known as the soul urge number, dictates what your deepest desires are. This number tells you what you truly feel and want, even though you might not know it.

More often than not, we choose not to confront this darker part of our personalities we don't even realize is a part of us. However, just like any other person, we too have our own hidden desires and instincts we like to keep personal and hidden from the outside world.

The heart's desire number reveals your motives and intentions in life. Knowing your soul urge number is important for you as it will show you the inclinations to which you are naturally predisposed. These greatly affect your career, family, love life, and even the kind of people to whom you are drawn. Overlooking it is a grave mistake as the heart's desire number provides one with a greater, deeper understanding of themselves.

Finding Your Heart's Desire Number

Finding your heart's desire number is similar to the procedure employed for all other numbers, except with one change. We will not be using the values of consonants but rather the vowels in our names.

There is a valid reason for that since vowels are considered the hidden aspects that provide meaning to any word. Likewise, the heart's desire number is a hidden aspect that greatly influences a person's life.

Contrary to vowels, consonants are more tangible and work as a shell that your exterior personality is akin to. This is why only vowels are used to discover this soul urge number, which is a deeper and more insightful number influencing our decisions.

For instance, let's find out the Heart's Desire Number for the name Snow White. But, first, we will write down all the vowels of this name and then associate them with their respective value, as shown in the table below:

A	E	I	O	U	Y
1	5	9	6	3	7

Using the table, we can conclude that Snow White has these values:

S	N	O	W	W	H	I	T	E
-	-	6	-	-	-	9	-	5

We can now add all of the values for the different vowels in the name:

6+9+5 = 20 (double digit so 2 + 0) = 2

The Heart's Desire Number for Ms. Snow White is 2. All we have to do now is reference this number to its description below. Once we check the qualities and pitfalls for number 2, we will easily discover our own personalities' desires, instincts, and motivations.

However, before we do that, we need to understand how Y functions in this case. People with a Y in their names must be confused about calculating their Heart's Desire Number. Let's look at how to overcome this issue.

How to Account For a "Y" in a Name

We can delve into this topic and make this unnecessarily complicated, or we can use the golden rule of phonetics to our advantage. The second option is better since it's usually correct and makes things easier.

If the Y in your name sounds like a vowel, then it is a vowel. Otherwise, it will be treated just like any other consonant. For example, in the name "Murray," the Y does not sound like a vowel- like it does in "Audrey." If the Y in your name sounds like a vowel, then assign it the value 7 and move on to the next step.

Heart's Desire Number Interpretations

After completing the above steps, you can come up with your Soul Urge Number. Now, this number is virtual if you don't have a clue what it represents. So, let's delve deeper into what the different numbers signify and which aspects of your inner self are revealed by each Heart's Desire Number.

Number 1

You are an independent person, and your desire to lead is overpowering. You don't like taking orders and thoroughly enjoying a challenging position to lead other people. In addition, you are extremely knowledgeable, which makes others want to follow you and ask for guidance.

You might sometimes become overconfident in your abilities and act arrogantly. This is something that people around you are not very fond of. However, if you can overcome this flaw in your attitude, you can become a leader who everyone willingly follows.

Your desire for independence means you take responsibility for your actions, and you believe in forging your life path, not playing by anyone else's rules. Your ambition and good judgment help you along the way by supporting your bold choices, which can be quite daring.

Number 2

You are a naturally loving and caring person who likes to maintain a sense of harmony in life. Your peacekeeping attitude is what motivates you to act as a pacifier in tense situations. You seek a balance in everything you do.

Since your emotions are what drive you, you easily fall in love. Your intuition helps you deal with people personally, which is why you excel at persuasion. Since your emotions rule you, tears can easily roll off your eyes, and you get vulnerable sometimes, which might be used against you.

You have a lack of confidence and tend to shy away from confrontation. However, if you can handle this issue of low confidence and get a hold of your emotions, you can easily succeed in life thanks to your sense of diplomacy and compromise.

Number 3

You are the person who is the life of any party or conversation. People are naturally drawn to you due to your impressive communication skills. In addition, you are very creative and artistic, which also reflects in your interpersonal skills.

The best career paths for you are those where you can freely express your creativity. Being a poet, writer, musician, or actor is what you were destined to do. In addition, you are mentally and emotionally well balanced, making you highly resilient to any blow that life throws your way.

You are optimistic, sometimes overly so, even ignoring the problems staring at you. You are also prone to excessive talking when under pressure or stressed. You often lose focus on a single thing, but you have a very good chance of success if you can mitigate these minor issues.

Number 4

You thrive with order, and you actively try to organize all aspects of your life. You are a punctual, dedicated, reliable, and trustworthy person. All these qualities ensure that you will make a good employee and a great parent.

You like to establish routines and cannot stand sudden changes to your daily life. For you, life does not get boring once you establish a regular routine. You like the safety and comfort of a regimen, and your life mostly revolves around your work. But if you are not careful, you might end up neglecting your family and social life.

You avoid taking risks due to your stable nature, and you sometimes appear to be dominating. However, your intentions are always good, and you just want to show your affection through your actions. If you can get better in touch with your emotions and express them more openly, others will be more receptive towards you.

Number 5

You are a free spirit who doesn't like being tied down in any way. Your love for exploration stems from your wanting to experience everything life has to offer. Meeting new people, visiting new places, and embarking on thrilling adventures excite you to the core.

You can be exceptionally inspirational to others thanks to your conversational skills and sharp intellect. However, your love for exploration prevents you from settling down in one place or in a relationship. You often worry about being held down if you commit yourself to someone. This is why you might start looking for a way out as soon as things get serious.

You are also adaptable and versatile, meaning you can easily adjust to new environments or people. But you are impatient and have a tendency not to see things through. This is why you should be careful in choosing what you want to pursue since a career you are genuinely passionate about will be the most suitable. You might want to look into arrangements like freelancing, remote work, and any other options that will guarantee you freedom and flexibility.

Number 6

You perhaps have the most loving and loyal attitude towards others, which is one of your core strengths. You sacrifice your comfort to spare the ones you love from having to go through any discomfort. The love and care you give others are also reciprocated since they deeply appreciate your devotion and selfless nature.

You are very devoted to family life and invest a lot of time and care to make it work. However, the overprotective nature you might exhibit towards your children can hinder their personal growth as you will always prevent them from learning lessons the hard way.

You might also suffocate others around you by constantly interfering in their lives. While your intentions will be pure and your actions come from good faith, you might get too overbearing. If you can control the urge to help everyone, then you will be much better off and successful in your endeavors.

Number 7

You are a scholar at heart who loves pondering over and deciphering the mysteries of the universe. You might be reserved and keep to yourself most of the time, which allows you to spend more time analyzing subjects that elude your understanding.

You have an insatiable thirst for knowledge, and it is never enough for you, no matter how much more you learn. You need to interact with people more and show your vulnerabilities to be more approachable. If you can adapt to new situations and take an interest in other people's lives, it will make your personality a more well-rounded and likable one.

Number 8

You live and breathe for one singular purpose, namely, to achieve success in your life. You do this because you desire power, prestige, and financial stability to be at your disposal. This is not entirely a bad thing, but you may get overly materialistic, self-centered, and dominating over others.

You have exceptional leadership skills and motivate others to give their best. You can also excel at managerial and administrative positions, but you often overlook instances where you'd need someone else's help. If you can become more attentive and self-reliant, your output will dramatically increase.

Your emotions are always in check, and nothing can faze you, but this becomes a drawback when you come across as overly stubborn and emotionless.

Number 9

You are a true humanitarian who wishes to put yourself at the service of humanity. You are often too idealistic for your own good, and you want to free the world of its sufferings and sorrows. You are a gentle and compassionate soul who believes there is no calling greater than service to others.

You have high ideals, but you are also naive and not a good judge of character. This fault in your judgment can affect you negatively and get you hurt and betrayed by people.

You must find a balance between service to others and your own comfort, as both are equally important. If you can control your emotions and let go of things, your life will prove much easier in the long run.

Number 11

You are a visionary who sees the world in a utopian state. You are idealistic and prefer to live your life this way despite the challenges. Your definition of what's right and wrong is solidly anchored in your mind, which can lead to unwanted conflict with others. And since conflict is against your nature, this can quickly demotivate you.

You probably were born in poverty and disadvantaged conditions, as is common with 11s. But this part of your upbringing taught you valuable lessons and made you stronger. You are a highly spiritual person who likes to think a lot, constantly trying to make sense of yourself, the world, and others.

If you can learn to control your emotions and accept the opinions of others, you will have a much easier time maintaining the harmony you seek.

Number 22

You are a creative and intelligent individual who wants to leave their mark on the world. You are a visionary ahead of your time and feel the need to be the best in whatever you do.

You undeniably have great strength hidden inside you. Combined with strong ambition and ideas, this will help you fulfill your dreams.

You can try to be less dominating and gentler in your approach. However, you might also get tensed due to overthinking, and it will help you if you try not to control every aspect of your life.

Number 33

You are a family-oriented person whose wish is a happy and healthy family life. You also want to be of service to others since you are full of compassion. You will be satisfied if you can manage to match your career with your desire to help out those in need. Some possible career options for you are social service, medicine, psychiatry, or similar profession that allow you to interact with people and improve their health and wellbeing.

You are loyal and caring, which makes you an excellent partner in romantic relationships. Your passion and emotions often move others, and people are inclined to handing you great responsibilities you may not want yourself.

Embracing your responsibilities and leading others will ensure that you bring change to the world you have always desired. If you run away from leadership roles, you might never bring in concrete change.

These were the associated qualities with each Heart's Desire Number. If you have carefully found your number, you are not aware of the qualities hidden inside of you.

We all have multiple qualities and issues embedded deep inside of us. Sometimes, even we are not aware of our own strengths and weaknesses. By knowing which aspects of our personalities we need to work on, we can actively resolve those issues.

This chapter was designed to ensure that you don't miss out on opportunities to improve and refine the hidden parts of your personality. After all, you cannot fulfill your destiny unless you fully know your own self.

Part Three: How Tarot Meets Astrology and Numerology

Chapter 10: What Is Tarot?

Tarot cards are quite the rage in the fields of astrology and numerology. Derived from the word "trionfi" (later known as "tarock" or "tarocchi"), tarot is a set of cards that have been in use since the 15th century in Europe. Today, people use tarot cards to delve deep into a person's intuition and provide wisdom and truth. In fact, it is a simple tool to learn more about one's life, personality, and achievements.

Cultural and Historical Background of Tarot

As mentioned, tarot cards were first used in parts of Europe starting from the mid-15th century by the Italian, Austrian, and French. Tarot cards were originally used as playing cards by wealthy families in Italy as they were mostly hand-painted and extremely expensive. While some enjoyed playing, others rebelled due to the toxic nature of gambling. However, it was only in the late 1700s that tarot cards were used for spiritual and divinity purposes. Frenchman Jean-Baptiste Alliette published a tarot card reading guide to tap into one's intuitive nature. He backed them up with astronomy and the teachings of Thoth, the Egyptian god of wisdom. In 1909, the cards were illustrated and developed in several versions ever since.

How Do Tarot Cards Work and How Can They Be Used?

Each tarot card carries its own unique weight and significance. Each symbolism or imagery describes a spiritual lesson and denotes a different meaning. A tarot deck comprises 78 cards: 22 of which are Major Arcana cards, and 56 of which are Minor Arcana cards. Upon drawing a tarot card, you can unleash your hidden story. It is believed that tarot cards act as a mirror to one's soul and represent their life story. Thus, when you pick and hold a card in your hand, you can reflect deep into your subconscious mind and harvest valuable insights into your life.

While Major Arcana cards represent the bigger picture, Minor Arcana cards can reveal details of one's daily life. To use tarot cards for reading, shuffle the deck and cut it in half. For beginners, starting with a one-spread reading is best. First, pick a card and turn it upside down. Then, refer to the representation of tarot cards to know what they mean. With time, you can practice different spreads (laying out the cards in specific patterns) and read your fortune or life lessons. Note that every card can be reversed (placing it upside down), which symbolizes the opposite of the actual meanings we will later discuss.

Major Arcana Cards

Major Arcana cards teach spirituality and convey lessons based on karma and eternity. The set of 22 cards represents one's life and the different phases they are likely to go through. The guidance, lessons, and perspectives these cards offer can help a person reach better awareness and live a more rewarding life. The bigger picture can be unraveled using these 22 cards. Let's take a brief look at the Major Arcana cards in tarot.

Card 0: The Fool

Mantra: New beginnings, a leap of faith, and a fresh start

Element: Air

Planet: Uranus

Chakra: Crown

Significance: Among all archetypes of the tarot set, the Fool card is extremely vulnerable due to its lack of experience and inability to distinguish right from wrong. He has not been through the ups and downs of life, thereby keeping him from deciphering his strengths, weakness, and future challenges.

Card 1: The Magician

Mantra: Skill, resources, and power

Element: Air

Planet: Mercury

Chakra: Throat

Significance: This card represents uniqueness and reminds you of your talents. The skills you possess are rare, and not everyone is blessed with your same talents. This helps you stand out from others and guides you on a successful path. This card shows you can overcome adversity, and it tells you to move forward in life with your skills.

Card 2: The High Priestess

Significance or Mantra: Sacred knowledge, higher wisdom, and intuition

Element: Water

Planet: Moon

Chakra: Third Eye

Significance: Among all cards, the High Priestess represents strong intuition and awareness. If you pick this card, you must listen to your instincts and follow your inner voice. Your mind can achieve anything and can seek answers to even the most difficult questions. All you must do is look inside instead of focusing on the outside world.

Card 3: The Empress

Mantra: Femininity, nurturing, beauty, abundance, and fertility

Element: Earth

Planet: Venus

Chakra: Heart and sacral

Significance: Symbolizing femininity and beauty, the Empress card hints at compassion in your life. Her deep-seated roots with Mother Nature motivate you to absorb the positive energies around you.

Card 4: The Emperor

Mantra: Establishment, authority, and father figure

Element: Fire

Planet: Mars/Aries

Chakra: Root

Significance: The authoritative status of the Emperor is achieved only after one has gone through hardships. Qualities like solidity, structure, and power are innately represented by this card, which tells you of your own strength. It encourages you to unravel your own inner strength and establish a powerful legacy.

Card 5: The Hierophant

Mantra: Religious beliefs, spiritual wisdom, and group identity

Element: Earth

Planet: Venus/Taurus

Chakra: Throat

Significance: As a messenger from above, the Hierophant card signifies religious and spiritual beliefs and guides people towards enlightening. Upon drawing this card, you must explore different forms of spiritual lessons you encounter and shape your current situation to expect the best outcome. In other words, pay attention to the rules to achieve the best results.

Card 6: The Lovers

Mantra: Harmony, love, relationships, bonds, and unions

Element: Air

Planet: Mercury/Gemini

Chakra: Heart

Significance: This card represents the relationships and close bonds in your life. If you pick this card during your reading session, you may have to focus more on your love life and try to strengthen your bonds. This card also represents your decisions and values, which is why you should also focus on these two aspects. When stuck at a crossroads in life, you must consider all the choices presented to you and decide after reflecting on the consequences.

Card 7: The Chariot

Mantra: Victory, success, control, momentum, and assertion

Element: Water

Planet: Moon/Cancer

Chakra: Throat

Significance: The Chariot card symbolizes determination, momentum in life, and natural drive and indicates success or victory soon. Once you learn to explore the power of your spirit and heart and combine it with your mental skills, you will be unstoppable in achieving all your goals. However, you also need the vigor to embark on the journey and triumph in the end.

Card 8: Strength

Mantra: Self-control, courage, strength, compassion, and influence

Element: Fire

Planet: Sun/Leo

Chakra: Solar Plexus

Significance: As the name suggests, this card represents the strength and courage that are probably hidden and need to be unveiled. This card represents courage and your heart's fortitude. If you are strong, you can achieve anything you want and withstand adversity alone. When caught in an intense situation, your power will help you move mountains and come out stronger than ever before.

Card 9: The Hermit

Mantra: Solitude, soul-searching, inner guidance, and introspection

Element: Earth

Planet: Chiron/Virgo

Chakra: Third Eye

Significance: When faced with a dire situation, you must be patient and listen to your inner voice by staying silent. Since the Hermit prefers to live alone, it is important to withdraw from the chaos of the outer world and figure out your life in solitude. This will enable you to anticipate any negative consequences in your life.

Card 10: The Wheel of Fortune

Mantra: Turning a cycle, karma, destiny, and good luck

Element: Fire

Planet: Jupiter

Chakra: Solar plexus

Significance: Life is an unpredictable ride. You will remain at the top at times, but some situations may suppress you. This is the significance of life. Nothing is permanent, and consequences may change with time. There is nothing too good or bad. If you are currently at the bottom, you will soon experience the better things in life. But if you are at the top, life can push you down without warning. So, be humble and willing to learn from the process.

Card 11: Justice

Mantra: Cause and effect, fairness, justice, law, and truth

Element: Air

Planet: Venus/Libra

Chakra: Heart

Significance: This card declares that karma is real, meaning every action will have a reaction. Justice is fair to everyone and does not discriminate. The decisions you made in the past can affect your current life, and your present actions determine your current state. Upon receiving this card during your reading session, note that your intuition points towards fair interaction and reinstating your actions with others. It is not too late to make a significant change.

Card 12: The Hanged Man

Mantra: Suspension, surrender, new perspectives, and pause

Element: Water

Planet: Neptune

Chakra: Third Eye

Significance: Sometimes, it is best to let go to benefit you in the long run. Even though small sacrifices may bother you at the moment, you will thank yourself for making them. If your life isn't going as planned and you pick the Hanging Man card, you must take a step to turn it around. However, not knowing where to start can halt you right from the beginning. The key is to let go of the situation to let yourself loose and avoid getting attached again.

Card 13: Death

Mantra: Beginnings, transformation, change, endings, and transition

Element: Water

Planet: Pluto/Scorpio

Chakra: Heart

Significance: This card represents the end of a phase in one's life and the beginning of a new one. Most people misunderstand this card as they assume it refers to physical death, which is entirely wrong. By hanging on to old relationships, situations, feelings, and emotions, you will not leave room for new and better things to come in your life. Make peace with the fact that every ending will have a well-deserved new beginning.

Card 14: Temperance

Mantra: Healing, balance, purpose, moderation, and patience

Element: Fire

Planet: Jupiter/Sagittarius

Chakra: Solar Plexus

Significance: Do not force change in your life, but instead, give it time to unfold in its own mysterious ways. You must master the art of moderation and be patient at the same time. Go with the flow and be peaceful along the way. Accept the things, ideas, and people coming into your life and welcome change. Condition yourself to remain flexible and adapt to new situations.

Card 15: The Devil

Mantra: Restriction, bondage, attachment, addiction, and sexuality

Element: Earth

Planet: Saturn/Capricorn

Chakra: Root

Significance: If you pick The Devil card during your reading, you may be feeling stuck. The fear and helplessness add to this chaotic feeling. Your life ahead may also seem bland due to a lack of opportunities and the unwillingness to explore your inner talents. This can also limit you from moving forward and exploring new situations because of low enthusiasm or self-confidence. While you do have the key to unlock new doors, the inability or unwillingness to do so can set you back tremendously.

Card 16: The Tower

Mantra: Sudden change, chaos, awakening, revelation, and upheaval

Element: Fire

Planet: Mars

Chakra: Crown

Significance: This card represents destruction and is dreaded by all. It showcases a person's misery and the phenomenon of their crumbling life. The person is also helpless and cannot control the situation. The Tower tells them to let it all fall to build anew. At times, all a person can do is let the weak parts tear down and start on a new basis. This restarting phase will last longer and stand more strongly.

Card 17: The Star

Mantra: Spiritual guidance, hope, purpose, faith, spirituality, and renewal

Element: Air

Planet: Uranus/Aquarius

Chakra: Crown

Significance: This card symbolizes hope and optimism. It shows how the universe is gathering all its positive energy to breathe good change in your life. It also tells you to keep the faith and let the universe do its job.

Card 18: The Moon

Mantra: Mystery, illusion, dreams, intuition, fear, and anxiety

Element: Water

Planet: Neptune/Pisces

Chakra: Third Eye

Significance: The Moon represents the subconscious that carries all your thoughts, fears, emotions, and doubts. A person drawing the Moon card in their reading is likely to feel anxious all the time, which can hinder their progress and performance. They let their fears and doubts get the best of them. Everything you see or hear may not be true, but if you focus on the positive, you can eliminate your fears and doubts.

Card 19: The Sun

Mantra: Vitality, youth, success, warmth, positivity, and fun

Element: Fire

Planet: The Sun

Chakra: Solar plexus

Significance: This card represents positivity and vitality in your life, which means that things are going well at the moment. Your thoughts, feelings, and path are well aligned and point in an obvious direction. You are surrounded by good people and things, which you must be grateful for.

Card 20: Judgment

Mantra: Inner calling, rebirth, and absolution

Element: Fire

Planet: Pluto

Chakra: Crown

Significance: The Judgment card represents your life as determined by your past actions and reflects the future. It tells you to check your progress and see whether or not it aligns with your future goals. Then, reflect on your actions to achieve your dreams. Your future can be changed by handling the present well. So, make it favorable and cherishable.

Card 21: The World

Mantra: Accomplishment, completion, integration, and travel

Element: Earth

Planet: Saturn

Chakra: Root

Significance: As the last card of this series, the World card represents the fulfillment and completion of your final goals. It means you are exactly where you are supposed to be in life. Your past experiences and lessons have taught you well, and you are fully prepared to enter the next phase of your life.

Minor Arcana Cards

The Minor Arcana cards represent tales and experiences of daily life based on tribulations and trials.

The main structure of the Minor Arcana comprises four suits, namely Wands, Pentacles, Swords, and Cups. They are further divided into numbers from 1 (Ace) to 10, including jacks, knights, queens, and kings.

Wands: The Wands suit represents your passion, motivation, and energy. Your ideas, spiritual status, and life purpose can be unraveled by picking this suit during your Tarot card reading session.

Pentacles: This suit depicts your material possessions and finances. The Pentacles suit can help you gather better insights into your professional career, wealth, and future opportunities.

Swords: The Swords suit represents your actions, thoughts, and words. The way you make decisions, communicate your ideas, and talk about your purpose in life all fall under this suit. It teaches you to assert your power, turn things in your favor, and communicate your thoughts openly.

Cups: This fourth and final suit represents creativity, intuition, and emotions. If you are facing emotional issues of any sort with your close ones, you are likely to get this suit during your tarot reading.

As we've seen, tarot readings can reveal a lot about your past, present, and future self. While the Major Arcana cards are mostly related to spiritual matters, the Minor Arcana cards relay aspects such as your career, business, and ambitions. The suits you pick can help you understand various areas of your life.

Chapter 11: The Fire Signs and Their Tarot Cards

The astrological connection with tarot cards can be drawn from the "Hermetic Order of the Golden Dawn," which dates back a few centuries. Although the basic learning structures of astrology were defined centuries ago, they are still intact and act as a base for fortune-telling. But tarot cards were revised during the Renaissance period, which may not provide enough leverage. However, since the same astrological learnings were used to reimagine tarot cards during the 1700s, we can draw parallels between both domains. This goes to show that the connection between zodiac signs and Tarot cards is strong and persuasive.

Fire signs (Aries, Leo, and Sagittarius) are intricately connected to their Major and Minor Arcana cards. The Major Arcana cards are associated with the layout of planets and related astrological readings. They are further broken down and placed as an elemental grouping known as the Minor Arcana group. This showcases the connection of Major Arcana and Minor Arcana groups with zodiac signs. They thrive harmoniously and share the same energy, which resonates well with their personality and upbringing.

In this chapter, we will explore Fire signs and their association with respective tarot cards.

Fire Signs

Fire signs represent warmth, brightness, and light. You need light and warmth to survive and make life more interesting and exciting. Fire signs are also vital and live to the fullest, spreading joy around them. Most crave attention but do not accept this. Some even do it without realizing it. Regardless, they always make the lives of people better and more cheerful. This is because they are extroverted and know that their bright presence can make someone's day. Fire signs stand by the idiom, "to light a fire under someone."

Fire Signs and the Suit of Wands

The suit of Wands represents qualities like willpower, action, and creativity. The tarot Wands are associated with Fire signs. This Minor Arcana card is closely related to the three zodiac signs in terms of attributes such as strength, intuition, determination, energy, creativity, expansion, and ambition. As Fire signs are full of light and wildness, the suit of Wands conforms to the zodiac signs. They are also hot, energetic, unpredictable, and wild. The way this suit represents your life and life lessons depends on how you leverage the qualities of the Fire sign. For instance, just like using fire to cook can be a productive and creative task, overuse can cause the food to burn. Likewise, the way you use your qualities will determine whether you excel in life.

The qualities displayed by the suit of Wands (corresponding to the Fire signs) are enthusiasm, personality, and internal and external personal energy. On the other hand, some negative qualities are impulsiveness, ego, illusion, and a lack of purpose. Thus, even though Fire signs are closely connected, they have their own distinct characteristics that set them apart. As such, each of the three zodiac signs expresses its traits in peculiar ways.

Aries (Mar 21 - Apr 19)

The most prominent trait of this zodiac sign is their leadership skills paired with their action-oriented personality. This zodiac sign is associated with the Ram, which is ambitious and bold.

Personality Traits of Aries

The Fire sign compels Aries to be enthusiastic and seek new activities in their life with others around them. However, they can be the victim of a strong ego and often display signs of self-obsession. But regardless of the challenges ahead, Aries will dive right in and overcome all the threats to come out victorious. Combined with their willpower and motivation, their passion allows them to excel in whatever they do, which can be attributed to the fire that blazes within them.

On the negative side, their perfectionism and relentlessness can become quite frustrating. This often leads them to work quickly and in haste. They act first and think later, which can bring about unwanted repercussions. This also teaches them multiple lessons as they move forward in life. According to popular legends, rams are extremely courageous and ready to fight in battles, which is why they were often armed. The fiery nature is apparent in Aries, but it doesn't last long and dissipates quickly.

Aries and Its Tarot Cards

Aries is represented by the Emperor and the King of Wands cards.

The Emperor

This card suggests that the Emperor will always be by your side, especially during critical times when you need him most. It says that your sign is loyal and that you will always stick close to your loved ones. Whenever your friends and family need someone by their side, you will be there and help them out. Basically, you are always on the clock, and your loved ones can rely on you through thick and thin. Since the Emperor also embodies power and authority, it asks you to dig deeper and unravel your true potential to establish a system and act as a strong support figure for your family.

Your analytical skills can also help you endorse this role and get closer to your goals. Just like Aries is placed first in the astronomical chart, the fire sign shows the first spark as the fire ignites. Since Aries are usually aggressive in nature and display leadership qualities, the Emperor perfectly suits this fire sign. This also has to do with the fact that the ram is authoritative and possesses a straightforward approach.

The King of Wands

The Minor Arcana card, the King of Wands, is also closely connected to Aries. Both are powerful, tough, and honorable. The King's throne displays power and honor, just like this zodiac sign. The King's confidence and control displayed by his wand are also seen in Aries. The fire energy, strength, and ability to conquer are other fire sign and Minor Arcana card qualities. Every motive in both domains is persistent and masculine. The dominant side of this sign also makes Aries take charge and resolve many issues in their personal and professional lives.

The King of Wands and Aries both abide by the motto "action speaks louder than words," which they prove time and again. Unlike other signs, Aries shows a strong connection with its tarot cards while retaining nuances of similarity. This Minor Arcana card illustrates the King's throne with lizards, salamanders, and lions, which signifies power. However, the King is portrayed as not sitting comfortably and wanting to move in haste, another characteristic of Aries. Overall, the throne and his ensemble represent his authoritative stance and pride in being king.

Leo (July 23 - Aug 22)

Leo has a charismatic and fiery nature as a zodiac sign thanks to its ruling planet, the Sun.

Personality Traits of Leo

Represented by the Lion, the Leo is mighty, ferocious, and the center of attention. Individuals with this zodiac sign often crave attention and being in the limelight. They can be either too dramatic or extremely loving. Most Leos possess both characteristics and balance them out. Just like a fire's flamboyant nature, this zodiac sign is also lively and willing to go to any extent to gain recognition. Like a fire that dances and shines brightly, Leos captures this essence in their personality and stays dynamic around the clock.

With the Sun as their ruling planet, a Leo personality remains the same throughout their life and changes only slightly. Their traits are apparent and stand out when compared to other signs. Leos need the center stage and have no issues stating so openly. They are not afraid to ask what they want and crackle like a blazing fire wherever they step. Furthermore, they are compassionate and warm to their loved ones. They can go to great lengths to protect their close friends and family members. Last, they possess leadership qualities and are extremely passionate, just like Aries.

Leo and Its Tarot Cards

Leo is represented by the Knight, Strength, and The Queen of Wands cards.

Strength

This card symbolizes a person's strength, both physical and mental. Like the mighty Lion who represents Leo, you can use your strength and courage to support and help your loved ones overcome obstacles. It denotes that nothing is impossible and that all you need is grit to accomplish your goals. You can also unleash your spiritual and emotional prowess to remain strong and resilient.

The Strength card is illustrated with the Lion, who seems bold and courageous, similar to Leo. The colors used in this card (mostly shades of golds and yellows) are also quite enigmatic and bright, just like the personality of this zodiac sign.

The physical and mental strength of a Leo is connected with the Strength card, represented by a gentle maiden patting the Lion. Leo's passionate personality rules hearts, which can be seen from the loving bond between the maiden and the Lion. Furthermore, the regal ensemble of the maiden in a white robe depicts the zodiac sign's progressive qualities such as honor, royalty, and bravery. The crown and floral sash she wears validate this representation.

The connection can also be ciphered through the Roman numeral 8 shown atop the card. Note that the 8th month of the year, August, is majorly represented by the Leo, which corresponds to the tarot deck's 8th card, Strength. Look closely, and we notice an infinity symbol floating in the sky above the maiden. It closely resembles the number eight, denoting another linkage. Since this number also represents generosity, karmic energy, and enthusiasm, the tarot card and zodiac sign are ideal portrayals of the infinity symbol. As you can see, the Strength tarot card and the Leo sign share a unique connection.

The Knight of Pentacles

Although this Minor Arcana card shares its qualities with Fire and Earth signs, the similarities between the Knight of Pentacles and the Leo are quite apparent. The force exerted by the Earth sign and the flaming desire of the fire sign bestows the card a traditional sense that keeps it grounded. The Knight of Pentacles is the archetype of leadership skills and confidence, reflected in Leo.

Furthermore, the Knight of Pentacles is cautious of his direction and advances carefully. This helps him reach his goals with a practical approach, thereby achieving success within the designated timeframe. He is ambitious and lets others depend on him, just like a true Leo would. Note that the intense energy represented by this zodiac sign is, in a way, connected to this Minor Arcana card.

The Queen of Wands

This card comes second in the tarot deck, which proves its connection with the Leo sign due to its rank as the second astrological sign in the Fire series. Just like the King of Wands, this card represents courage, determination, and a strong-willed personality. The illustration on this Minor Arcana card depicts the Queen in a rich ensemble of bright red and yellow shades, showcasing the regal side of this wealthy sign.

With the lion heads on the Queen's throne and the feline creature by her side, the connection between the Leo and the Minor Arcana card is evident. While the Queen is courageous and powerful, she also has a kind face that makes her dependable. She will do anything for her kingdom's well-being, just like a Leo would when protecting their friends and family.

Sagittarius (Nov 22 - Dec 21)

The ruling planet of this zodiac sign is Jupiter and is often on the path of seeking pleasure and truth in equal bits.

Personality Traits of Sagittarius

As mentioned, this zodiac sign is always seeking truth, going to any length to make it happen. Even though they are joyful, they feel anxious upon remembering that nothing is permanent and that it will all end. At some point, they may delve deep into exploration, so much so they may start feeling overwhelmed. When it comes to sharing their views, they can be dogmatic. This is because the melancholy of everyday life and the fear of not finding answers can push them into a dilemma and even in terror.

Sagittarius and Its Tarot Cards

Sagittarius is represented by the Temperance and the Page of Wands cards.

Temperance

You are abundantly blessed with mediation skills, which means you can draw parallels between situations and find common ground to feel at ease. You are self-aware and possess a genuine understanding of your life's whereabouts, which can balance them out of judgments. Your patience and diligence can help you get through hardships and pave the way to brighter days. You are like a meandering stream capable of clearing its way to flow smoothly. Temperance is linked to balance and is extremely curious of its surroundings. In fact, every form of astrological relation associated with the Sagittarius represents its need to find and thrive on enlightenment. Although the Sagittarius sign has learned and gathered enough information, they continue to question their surroundings to strengthen their knowledge.

While the Sagittarius is a fire sign, they are on the verge of turning into smoke due to their curiosity and potential for stagnation. This is vaguely represented by the angel on the Temperance card who tries to balance the flowing water in both cups, the unending process of finding knowledge, contentment, and solace.

The Page of Wands

This Minor Arcana card represents impulse, enthusiasm, cleverness, and courage, much like the fire sign Sagittarius. The robes of the character on the card represent the Fire sign, which has similar qualities to the salamander on the Queen and King cards. The word "new" resonates well with the Page of Wands as they always seek new pursuits and philosophical perspectives, yet another similar quality shared by this zodiac sign.

When reading your horoscope, consider your sign and tarot card as a whole to gain a deeper perspective of your life and intuition. This will also help you be more knowledgeable when practicing tarot cards and horoscope reading. With time, you will notice the significance of the Fire signs in their respective tarot cards and vice versa. You will also get a clearer picture of your motives and direction towards a brighter future.

Chapter 12: The Earth Signs and Their Tarot Cards

As you learned, zodiac signs are divided into four elemental groups: Fire, Earth, Air, and Water. In the previous chapter, we discussed Fire signs and their association with respective tarot cards. Let's now jump on to the Earth signs, perhaps the most "down-to-earth" of all zodiac groups. Their level-headedness and practicality are desirable qualities that attract other signs to the Earth group. However, even though they are observed in other signs, it is the way they represent and showcase these qualities that set them apart.

In this chapter, we will talk about the Earth signs and their association with tarot cards.

Earth Signs

The Earth signs (Taurus, Virgo, and Capricorn) are the three zodiac groups representing individuals with the most practical approach towards their personal and professional lives. They focus more on materials and finances. Due to their nature, they are oriented towards physical health rather than mental or emotional health. All three signs are extremely hardworking and committed to their responsibilities. They are steadfast and will commit to changing their life by working hard. They can be patient, level-headed, and determined to chase their dreams and attain success.

While Earth signs are primarily stubborn, they can be equally practical as well. Certain qualities like patience and loyalty are also positive traits that Earth signs carry with pride. On the negative side, they can be inflexible and need things to go their way. They crave material things and can even get obsessed with them. This can also make them decadent and somehow lazy. When compared to other signs, they are the most grounded and realistic. While they are pragmatic most of the time, they can also portray signs of aggression and anger on bad days. When enraged, anyone should keep away from them.

Earth Signs and the Suit of Pentacles

The Pentacle suits (also known as the Coin suit), a part of the Minor Arcana tarot deck, are dedicated to Earth signs. Earth signs and the Pentacles suit represent anything related to materials, finances, and physical health. Every card associated with the Pentacle suit in the Minor Arcana deck reflects the traits of the Taurus, Virgo, or Capricorn sign. While some may represent a particular Earth sign, others provide subtle hints that make the tarot cards and zodiac signs extremely relatable. For example, the Four, Five, and Six of Pentacles symbolize money matters linked to Earth signs. While the Four and Six of Pentacles tell one to save and donate money, respectively, the Five of Pentacles hints at monetary losses in the near future.

As you can see, your card reading can also help Earth signs be prepared in financial and professional areas and make necessary changes to stay safe. Both the Earth signs and the Suit of Pentacles mirror various levels of consciousness with the creative and health aspects of an individual. The way a person creates and transforms their life also echoes with this suit of the tarot deck.

Taurus (April 20 - May 20)

The Taurus is known to be determined, strong-headed, and very stubborn in most aspects of their life.

Personality Traits of Taurus

The Ox represents the sign. Whether it's the clothes they wear or the food they eat, the Taurus likes the finer things in life. Deemed to be the artists among other Earth signs, the Taurus use their pleasures, artistic skills, and sensuality to inspire others and motivate their loved ones. They chase their dreams using this innate beauty and passion.

People can safely rely on individuals with this zodiac sign. They are stable, persistent, and work hard. However, on a bad day, they can be aggressive and lazy. They can even be possessive of their belongings and loved ones, which is a trait rarely displayed. Despite negative qualities like jealousy and possessiveness, they are loyal to their partners, friends, family members, and other loved ones. The Taurus is notorious by nature, and their flirting skills can get over the top. They pay extra attention to the ones they love and expect the same in return. All in all, they will go to any length to fulfill their dreams and live happily.

Taurus and Its Tarot Cards

Taurus is closely associated with the Hierophant, the Knight, and the King of Pentacles cards.

The Hierophant

In Greek, the Hierophant is known as "high priest" and is often called the Pope. This card is the leader of all tarot cards with its organization and holy nature. This card comes fifth in the series of the Major Arcana tarot deck. It represents positive qualities such as creativity and joy. The Hierophant is seen holding a triple specter in the left hand, showcasing domination. Basically, this card is a representation of power in the world of material things. It also preaches practicality and rules, something that the Taurus is known for.

With power, the Taurus can reach goals and chase dreams without feeling insecure or demotivated. They also govern some senses of the physical world, including pleasure and sensuality. Even though the Taurus takes their time, they can achieve great things with their inner power and creative flair. With time, they can even dominate the world. They are rightly called "the master creator." This zodiac sign is instantly attracted to individuals with knowledge and a spiritual nature. Since they appreciate discipline and hard work, the Taurus likes being validated and is therefore attracted to these qualities.

The Knight of Pentacles

All knights represent the Taurus' behavior and the life lessons they supposedly learn on their way. However, the Knight of Pentacles resembles the zodiac sign more than any other. Just like the Taurus can wait patiently to achieve their goals, the Knight of Pentacles is also steadfast and willing to wait until they see a desirable outcome. The card and the zodiac sign are down-to-earth yet stubborn. They will formulate a plan and stick to it until they are satisfied. Regardless of how much time it takes (possibly years), they will remain patient and virtuous throughout the journey.

On its tarot card, the Knight is depicted as a calm, self-assured character who seems to be perfectly in touch with the world around him. This card also stands for passion, freedom, and youth, which equates to the signs and behavior of the Taurus sign. However, the Knight can be slightly more deliberate and slower than its counterparts, especially the Knight of Wands and Swords. The Knight of Pentacles plans his moves, explaining why he is slower, just like a Taurus. He respectfully holds the Pentacle and appears to be wary of his actions. He also keeps the horse in control when seated, which shows a bright and confident demeanor.

His visual field is patiently gazed upon by the Knight, and he studies his vistas with scrutiny. He is ready to take on the world but quietly plans his moves. He patiently awaits the right moment to move ahead and conquer the world. Although he is dressed for combat, he will not take a single step until fully prepared. Furthermore, the black horse aligns with the Taurus' independent and mature self. The Knight can control the horse and battle through the hardships he faces. His perseverance and determination will keep him grounded and make his life easier.

This shows that the Taurus will take calculated risks and design a blueprint before embarking on a tough journey. This strategy will also make them more confident and mature. However, whenever the Taurus faces emergencies and attempts to sort them out, the Knight of Pentacles may act as an obstacle. In such cases, the Taurus must learn to think on their feet and make quick decisions to overcome the situation permanently.

Virgo (Aug 23 - Sep 22)

This zodiac sign is represented by the Maiden and is ruled by the planet Mercury.

Personality Traits of Virgo

As mentioned, Virgo covers the practical aspects of one's life, just like any of the Earth signs. The Virgo has an analytical mind and puts truth on a pedestal. Among other signs, they are the most practical and reasonable, which is why their loved ones often rely on them to make decisions. Their minds are naturally wired to make the most informed decisions. They can investigate circumstances with scrutiny and know that their minds can pull them out of the worst situations. On the negative side, the Virgo can obsess over the tiniest details, which can place them in a dilemma. In extreme situations, they may also ruin their life due to this obsession.

However, usually, their detail-attentive nature helps them stay aware and gather valuable knowledge. In fact, the Virgo prefer to stay this way to be able to adjust to change easily. Since they are loyal and sensible, they make excellent partners and have a strong social network. Their meticulousness helps them seek improvement in their personal and professional lives.

Virgo and Its Tarot Cards

Virgo is closely associated with the tarot cards the Hermit and the Queen of Pentacles.

The Hermit

This card can be deemed the closest to Virgo because it tells this zodiac sign's journey and highlights the most important parts. The Hermit is one of the most enlightened and spiritually aware cards in the tarot deck. Strong instincts and potent force are some qualities shared by the Virgo as well. The card states that if someone wishes to bring positive changes in their life, the key to achieving this goal lies within. They possess the power to make those changes successfully. The Virgo abides by a similar motto. They should take inspiration from this tarot card and reflect on their actions to breathe positive energy and wisdom into their life.

The Hermit also inspires this zodiac sign to share their knowledge and gain a better perspective to thrive with others. The Virgo may struggle to find their inner calling and true self. When they are on the path towards awareness and making peace with their consciousness, they may expect respect, patience, and space from the people around them. This is why the Virgo needs a partner who can understand them and respect their values. You should be able to have intelligent conversations with them and build healthy communication. The spiritual aspirations of the Hermit are lofty, and they resonate with the Virgo's spiritual side as well.

The Queen of Pentacles

While the Hermit represents the Virgo's spirituality, the Queen of Pentacles balances the zodiac sign's attributes with a less abstract approach to life. She is nurturing, resourceful, and warm-hearted, some signs the Virgo represents too. In a way, the Queen completes the other cards in the tarot deck, yet another shared attribute with the Virgo. Individuals with this zodiac sign complete the lives of their loved ones.

A major contradiction that the Hermit and the Queen of Pentacles present is the balance between spirituality and wealth. While some may seek solace on a spiritual path and become monks, others may pursue abundance and become wealthy. In the end, it all comes down to the individual's needs, aspirations, and thought pattern. For some, wealth can also be spiritual, thereby presenting a perfect amalgamation of both entities.

Capricorn (Dec 22 - Jan 19)

This zodiac sign is represented by the Sea-Goat, which is half fish and half goat.

Personality Traits of Capricorn

Commonly known as the originators of the Earth signs, the Capricorn is a hardworking group determined to stay focused and ambitious. They are proud and hold a stature in the society they live in. They prefer to have control over their life and establish a system to keep this arrangement in place. They chase the future and take the necessary steps to turn circumstances in their favor. However, this can deeply affect their emotions and sensitivity. The Capricorn will never be sidelined or stay in a single place, especially when they are not making steady progress in life. If they do find themselves lagging and lacking, they will take immediate action to turn it around.

Contrary to popular belief, the Capricorn will barely hold grudges and easily move on in life. For them, their career can surpass every other priority, even their personal life and relationships sometimes. They rarely give up and keep hard at work, building themselves a lifestyle that can make others envious. All three Earth signs are compatible and go well with one another. This is why they make great friends and long-term partners.

Capricorn and Its Tarot Cards

Capricorn is closely associated with the Devil and the Page of Pentacles cards.

The Devil

Much like the Capricorn who is fierce and speaks their heart, the Devil card is utterly savage and raw. The Devil card is intimately linked with Pan, the Greek god with a half-goat, half-man build. This connection also extends to the Capricorn, which can be extracted from Greek mythology. Both the Capricorn and the Devil want to live their wildest fantasies and go as far as possible. The Devil card feeds the Capricorn's raw desires fearing no dangerous outcome. This zodiac sign is also fearless and can go to any extent to fulfill their dreams.

Despite being tenacious and wild, the Devil is not ashamed of who he is. He lives proudly and believes that everyone must have a little bit of devil in them. In a way, the Capricorn can be just and unbiased for that reason. The Capricorn is also good in bed and desires a partner with similarly orgasmic skills. This card connects the zodiac sign with a partner who shares similar fantasies and expectations and can signify a healthy relationship for a Capricorn. If it pops up in your reading, you may be blessed with a committed and long-lasting relationship.

The Page of Pentacles

This Minor Arcana card symbolizes child-like attributes due to the Page's curious nature. He is a learner and an explorer. Once he finds something interesting, he will go in-depth and pore over the subject to the core. You can tell from the way he holds the Pentacle and gazes around with curiosity. Despite having the ability and resources, the Knight is unknot interested in ruling the kingdom and would rather explore his beautiful terrain and keep away from worries and dangers.

Chapter 13: The Air Signs and Their Tarot Cards

Air signs are the most committed and skilled with communication. The Gemini, Libra, and Aquarius make up the Air signs and keenly carry their stories through corresponding tarot cards. In the tarot deck, the Suit of Swords is the ideal representation of Air signs in terms of qualities, traits, and the manifestation of dreams. The cards also teach the air signs to act based on their current situation and condition.

In this chapter, we will talk about the Air signs and their association with respective tarot cards.

Air Signs

Air signs (Gemini, Libra, and Aquarius) are known as the doers and communicators among all signs. They possess an analytical mind and can synthesize any situation to retrieve the best outcome. They are fiery, restless, and always on the path of exploration seeking new adventures and information. You can try to stop an Air sign but will most likely fail. They are all about probing through life without catching their breath and chasing their dreams relentlessly. Since they are mostly asocial, they draw their own path in solitude without bothering others. For them, "live and let live" is the ultimate mantra.

Since Air signs are naturally intelligent and creative, they can make quick decisions that likely produce the best outcome. Even though they prefer to be alone, they have a communal sense of responsibility and do not shy away from suggesting effective solutions to better society. For them, practicality trumps emotions, and they are hardly clouded by the latter. Therefore, any kind of information retrieved and passed on by an Air sign is most probably correct and accurate. Since they live to achieve and produce new ideas, you can safely rely on them to make decisions and point out mistakes.

Air Signs and the Suit of Swords

The sword energy of the Minor Arcana cards represents Air signs, which signify action, vision, and intelligence. Since all three signs share the foundational energy of the Suit of Swords, they can easily decipher a person's inner thoughts and beliefs. This is important if the individual is uncertain about how their life is taking shape and where it is headed. Air signs are firm representatives of dual aspects, which illustrates a person's duality. Whether it's stability and intuition or intelligence and power, Air signs always manage to strike a balance between these qualities. If any imbalance is noted, the individual may benefit from too much positivity or suffer due to potential harm.

However, the Suit of Swords is not always auspicious in a tarot reading because of its proclivity for trouble. It can mean that the person is either too angry or prioritizes intelligence over other aspects, destroying their personal and social life. While the Suit of Swords primarily depicts air signs, some are also parts of the cups (discussed more below). This combined energy is often perceived as an element of curiosity and studied to extend it further.

Gemini (May 21 - June 20)

This zodiac sign is represented by the Twins, which reflects the dual personality of the Gemini.

Personality Traits of Gemini

Among all zodiac signs, the Gemini is perhaps one of the most flexible and energetic. They are so in tune with their inner selves that chaos or disorder can hardly put their livelihoods in disarray. They will prove calm and comfortable in almost every situation. The Gemini possesses a strange sense of perception they combine with reality. Usually, they fail to distinguish between reality and the fake realms they imagine in their minds.

Usually, this zodiac sign is social and pleases others with great charisma. They are restless by nature and often look for people to share their deep thoughts and conversations. They despise schedules and fail to stick to one. Generally, they do not plan their time in the first place as they know their free-spirited nature. The Gemini do as they please and don't like setting boundaries. Therefore, it is not surprising to see the Gemini spreading their positive energy everywhere around them. Moreover, they do not hold themselves back and are not afraid to speak their mind.

Gemini and Its Tarot Cards

Gemini is closely associated with the Lovers and the King of Swords cards.

The Lovers

This tarot card is a strong representation of the Air sign as it represents their dual personality and intimacy. The Lovers exemplify "completing each other" or "sharing equal energy" to become one. The Lovers are charming and curious, which are also two apparent traits of the Gemini. This is also one reason others are attracted to individuals with this zodiac sign. The Lovers are physically attracted to each other and share the same emotional energy, making them the essential "other half." They possess every quality that a couple should have, including healthy communication, physical affection, and a flirtatious demeanor.

Just like the Gemini makes you feel extra special in a relationship, the Lovers fall head over heels for each other. They effectively redefine love and passion. Since the Gemini prefer not to stay alone, the Lovers further depict their dependent nature. They find solace in each other's arms and feel extremely comfortable, just as the Gemini does. This card speaks of love, harmony, union, and attraction, which balances one's sense of purpose and living. Whether it's in life or in love, the Gemini seeks balance above all.

The King of Swords

The King is a representation of authority and intelligence, which are two prominent qualities of the Gemini. If this card shows up in your reading, you may come to meet a person of high authority soon. Just like the Gemini, the King of Swords is on the path of seeking justice and truth. He likes to explore, much like the tarot card's counter zodiac sign. Even though the King means well, not everyone construes his intentions in a positive light. The card illustrates the King with a blank face where he lacks expression and is seen watching his land with curiosity.

When drawing this card, you might have already established order in your life or are working hard to get your life together. This quality can also be seen in the Gemini. They follow a specific method and draft a protocol to safeguard their situation. Due to their practical nature, you hardly see them getting emotional. In fact, they shape their emotions into realistic and practical aspects, which according to them, makes situations easier to control. This makes them rational and far-sighted by nature.

Libra (Sep 22 - Oct 23)

The Scales symbolize this zodiac sign, which stands for harmony and balance.

Personality Traits of Libra

Libras represent strong social connections and strive for love and cooperation from their friends and family. They are appreciated for their just and fair-minded attitude, which helps them make better decisions. They are intelligent and interesting beings who offer plenty of knowledge to those around them. However, the other signs should be open to seeking and receiving the wisdom of the Libra. Individuals with this zodiac sign are charming and often work on pre-established schedules. They want things to be in order and always seek balance in all aspects of their life.

The Libra knows how to compromise and can help resolve issues caused by misunderstandings or misjudgments. They know how to make peace with others. They are calm and give time to their partners and friends to speak up and resolve arguments. For this reason, Libras are known to make amazing friends, partners, and leaders. They learn from their own mistakes and apply those lessons in their personal and professional lives. While most Libras are exciting and likable, some may disappoint you. However, they often come clean due to their level-headedness, which makes them more reliable overall.

Libra and Its Tarot Cards

Libra is closely associated with the tarot cards Justice and the Queen of Swords.

Justice

As the name suggests, this card advocates for justice and fairness, just like Libra. It illustrates a judge holding scales in the left hand, which is the prime symbolization of balance most Libras seek. It showcases the intention of individuals who often employ their expertise and intuition to make important decisions and take necessary steps. As the 11th card in the tarot deck, Justice represents strong intuitive power, just like the number 11. The number is so powerful that it is commonly known as the "Master number" in the astrological world.

In parallel, the number 11 can be seen in the pillars illustrated on the tarot card, which strengthens the connection. Excessive usage of any aspect can cause an imbalance, which can frazzle the Libra. The Justice lady holds a double-edged sword in her other hand, which signifies protection against ambiguity or confusion. Any sort of conundrum can easily be cut with the sword. You can also relate the illustrated sword with the Suit of Swords, which represents all Air signs.

The Queen of Swords

The lady illustrated on this card represents solitude, something most Libras often seek. The Queen favors emotions over practical matters and prefers to live alone. She is also looking to solve all the problems that lie ahead, which explains her curious gaze. Her rationality and practical response can likely help her solve matters with her judicious skills. If you get this card in your reading, your intuition is pointing at your rational skills and encourages you to use them to make more informed decisions. It states that if you look deep enough, you can easily take charge of your life and find answers to your problems.

The Queen illustrated on the card appears emotionless yet still demonstrates a mild, curious gaze with a sword held upright. Her ensemble seems conservative, and her pose looks serious. Yet, she has integrity and stands with the truth. She probably doesn't need the support of a loved one as it can trigger her emotions. In fact, she would rather handle the situation and life challenges with tact and grace. Despite being critical and just, she will compel you to look deep inside and appreciate your own qualities.

Aquarius (Jan 20 - Feb 18)

This sign is represented by the aquatic animal, the water-bearer, and is ruled by the planet Uranus.

Personality Traits of Aquarius

Their quirky nature and eccentric personality often garner plenty of attention. Aquarians perceive themselves to be just and forthright. However, they can get absorbed in deep thinking, which is why they often get distracted. They are the prime example of mankind and abide by the law of the community. If you need someone by your side in times of need, an Aquarian will always reach out to help. However, they lack the ability to console others and provide reassurance. Since they focus more on the community instead of single individuals, they do not always expect to feel better in the company of an Aquarian.

Aquarians are often seen as detached from the world due to their own thought patterns. You need evidence and fact-based data to persuade an Aquarian to accept your viewpoint. Since they are known for going with the flow, changing their mindset can be quite a challenge. While deep thinking and self-reflection are positive qualities, usually, the Aquarius can prove annoying when they fail to listen to others and think about random subjects.

Aquarius and Its Tarot Cards

Aquarius is closely associated with the Star, the Knight, and the Page of Swords cards.

The Star

This card illustrates a woman holding a cup and pouring water into another water body deeply connected to the Earth. It represents nourishment and hope. It compels the sign to look forward to the future and be patient. The woman places one foot in the water body, which relates to the individual's intuition. To counterbalance this, she places another foot on the land. This means that the individual is stable yet intuitive at the same time.

Since the Aquarius is represented by water and air, this reference can help better understand the connection.

While the air element demonstrates the woman's intellect, the water depicts her emotional side. Furthermore, the Star represents the sign's traits of staying inspired and finding guidance while seeking solace in an oversaturated world. Aquarians prefer to stay alone and hardly blend in with the community, which can be seen from the single large star on the tarot card. Individuals with this sign are highly intuitive and can easily find their inner calling. They are guided by their gut feelings and listen to them carefully. Some highly depend on their intuition when making important decisions while dismissing external or practical opinions.

The card also shows a bird behind the woman known as the Sacred Ibis of thinking and thoughts. The bird is the representation of the element that sprouts our mind's tree. This also shows that the Aquarius is intelligent and can carve their own path in life with their strong intuition. In essence, the Star and the Aquarius zodiac sign share a sense of inspiration, societal improvement, and thriving on their intuition.

The Page of Swords

This Tarot card depicts a young man standing on a mountain peak with a sword in his hands. He is looking in the opposite direction and appears ready to use the sword. He looks young and prepared but is not exactly ready for combat. He wants to fight for his principle and beliefs, reflected in his confident, fearless look. However, it is not the right time for the Page to fight the world as he is not yet fully grown. If this card shows up in your reading, your mind and body are not prepared to deal with the challenge that lies ahead. You must be patient and let time take its course. Step back and experience the journey taking no risk. If not, you will waste your energy and time without gaining a favorable outcome.

All in all, Air signs adhere to community beliefs and carry a strong vision to make a difference in the world. However, certain life challenges can temporarily hinder their personal and outer world perspective, which can be resolved or at least handled by reading the corresponding tarot cards that pop up on their spread.

Chapter 14: The Water Signs and Their Tarot Cards

As you learned in the previous chapters, specific elemental groups are closely associated with a certain set of tarot cards. While some share qualities and traits with other signs, most adhere to specific signs, making tarot card reading easier. In the last group in discussion, the Water signs correspond to the emotional side of the tarot, which is the Suit of Cups. Since Water signs rule over their emotions, this suit perfectly embodies the traits of the three zodiac signs, namely Cancer, Scorpio, and Pisces.

In this chapter, we will talk about the water signs and their association with respective tarot cards.

Water Signs

Pluto, the Moon, and Neptune rule water signs (Cancer, Scorpio, and Pisces). Among all, individuals with the Water sign are the most sensitive and delicate through their emotions. At times, rational thinking can be quite challenging as they favor emotions over practicality. This is a major disadvantage for those who need to make informed decisions. Although individual characteristics vary from sign to sign and person to person, all Water signs can be labeled as creative, sensitive, and intuitive. In addition, they are compassionate beings who can easily make friends and stay loyal to their loved ones. Their sensitive and benevolent nature pulls them closer to their social group, which is why they are often the stars among their friends and family.

Furthermore, the water signs are extremely creative and often engage in artistic ventures. Not surprisingly, they make fantastic poets, writers, actors, and artists. Their strong psychic abilities and intuitive power are quite impressive. They can care and nurture, which is why they make great partners and parents. Their emotional side also makes them capable guardians who can take care of children with utmost diligence.

Water Signs and the Suit of Cups

As mentioned, Water signs and the suit of Cups are linked to each other. For them, love, relationships, feelings, connections, and emotions trump other qualities. The suit of Cups abides by a similar principle. Since water is agile and fluid, it can easily flow through or on any surface. It can take the shape of the container it is poured in and act. It can be molded as needed yet still be gentle. Regardless of how you treat water, it can either work for you or against you. For instance, it can show its power through massive, raging waves crashing on the shore or flow gently in the form of a brook.

Just like the Water sign, the suit of Cups can represent healing, fluidity, and cleansing. It is feminine, subtle, and powerful. Just like a woman, this suit declares its ability to adapt to change and take responsibility. It flows, nurtures, receives, and purifies. If you get the suit of Cups in your reading, you must be prepared to think rationally and with your head instead of your heart. Put your emotions aside and handle the situation with an analytical mind.

Cancer (June 21 - July 22)

This zodiac sign is represented by the Crab and ruled by the Moon.

Personality Traits of Cancer

The most prominent signs of Cancer are sensitivity and emotional attitude. They may seem firm and stubborn on the outside but are rather warm and soft on the inside. However, you must get very close to them to know their real side. They are notorious for being moody and wandering out of focus. The Cancer is self-aware but can still project a layered personality. For them, current emotions and sorrows will dictate the course of their lives. This can also affect the lives of their loved ones at all times. However, they will try to understand others and decipher their sorrows to make their loved ones feel lighter and better.

By contrast, they will barely open up to others. They carry this fear of being exposed or vulnerable, which is why they prefer to stay shut. They do not want others taking advantage of their pain and weaknesses and therefore stay isolated. Even if they are not well, they will act as if they are and convince others. This often pushes them into a downward spiral.

Cancer and Its Tarot Cards

Cancer is closely associated with the Chariot and the King of Cups cards.

The Chariot

The connection between Cancer and the Chariot fascinates tarot readers and astrologers because they display contradictory qualities. While the Cancer is known to be nurturing and kind towards their peers, the Chariot displays signs of progress and growth. Even though these two sets of qualities are not exactly opposite, they do not sit well with each other either. The Chariot card's representation of evolution and movement signals the individual towards needing to work on their intuitive growth and reflect on their movement. With this, the person can truly experience evolution and move forward in life.

The Chariot tells a person to dig deeper and find their true purpose to experience transformation. Just like the zodiac sign, the Chariot also asks us to tug on the strings of our hearts to strengthen intuitive power. If you get this card in your reading, you are probably going through a stagnant phase with no clear way out. However, you can pull yourself out of such a plateau by working on your beliefs and channeling your inner forces.

The King of Cups

As you learned, all the cards representing the suit of Cups show water in their illustrations, which showcases their connection with Water signs. One such card, the King of Cups, shows an emperor sitting on a throne that rests on a sea. The high waves cover the base of the throne by crashing into each other. The card also depicts a ship and a dolphin behind the throne. The waves and the sea, which symbolize a person's unconscious mind, seem quite turbulent. It means that the person should find the real reason behind their current hardship.

The King of Cups has Cancer as his zodiac sign, another connection between the two entities. The cards represent qualities such as love, romance, and financial independence, and a Cancerian can also display these qualities. In addition, they can take responsibility and handle crises with maturity. The King of Cups is also considerate and wary of other people's feelings. He is calm on the outside and soft on the inside. However, he can be moody at times. Some successful career paths include chef, minister, priest, doctor, or businessman.

Scorpio (Oct 23 - Nov 21)

This Water sign is deeply sensitive and also ruled by their emotions. Interestingly enough, they are represented by the Scorpio, which is a land animal.

Personality Traits of Scorpio

The Scorpio is perhaps the most peculiar and misunderstood among all signs. With their intimidating stance, they are often perceived as arrogant and mean. However, this need for having their own space is often misinterpreted. They are intimate, loyal, and make great friends. Having a Scorpio in your life is, in fact, a blessing. The Scorpio rules in social settings thanks to their strong and charming personality. Their presence is quite powerful, which is also why they can be intimidating. This is also due to their mysterious nature and penchant for puzzles.

The Scorpio seeks intimacy in all forms due to its emotional nature. Since they are serious and possess ruling abilities, they also make great and efficient leaders. They are also intense, which adds to the leadership. At times, they can come across as mean or rude. However, they just mean better for you and wish to see improvement in your life. They are also determined and can make the most out of the bare minimum. If they seek to achieve something, they will never return empty-handed. The Scorpio prioritizes their goals and goes to any length to fulfill them.

Scorpio and Its Tarot Cards

Scorpio is closely associated with the tarot cards Death, the Knight, and the Queen of Cups.

Death

Since the scorpion (Scorpio sign) is known to be a deadly animal, it is always connected to the Death card in the tarot deck. This is why most people who get this card in their reading often panic. While most relate this card to physical death, it actually emphasizes the true meaning of the life-death cycle and how this endless loop sustains human life. Basically, it means that every dark night is followed by a bright day and that the bad situation you are in will soon give way to happier days. This can also mean the opposite, in that nothing is permanent, and you must stay prepared for changing circumstances.

The Scorpio sign also depicts sexuality, a symbol of new life. This can be linked to the Death card that symbolizes rebirth. It is believed that individuals who draw this card in their reading should listen to their unconscious mind and spirit as it is asking them to find a higher purpose. Interestingly, the month of Halloween also coincides the Scorpio's birth month. Even though Halloween symbolizes death, most people celebrate it with joy and life.

The Knight of Wands

This card illustrates a knight in full armor ready to enter the battlefield. In the same way, the Scorpio is impulsive and ready to bite, so the Knight is also prepared to defeat his enemies. His ensemble comprises a bright yellow robe with flames over this armor. This is linked to the fiery nature of the Scorpio, who can bite to kill his enemies and protect themselves. The card also shows him holding a sword in this right hand that is raised high. This demonstrates the Knight's enthusiastic nature and swift movements. He is ready to move forward and conquer the land before him.

Like a Scorpio that glides in haste, the Knight is also believed to be full of energy and advance without thinking twice. Sometimes, this can be dangerous. If you get this card in your reading, it means you might find a new idea that might change your life. However, you must not make hasty decisions during execution as it can lead to failure. Prepare a solid plan and take it one step at a time. This card also tells you that you have enough courage and willingness to succeed in life and achieve your goals.

The Queen of Cups

This card illustrates a queen sitting on her throne, staring at a cup she is holding in one hand. She is deeply engrossed, trying to figure out the thoughts hidden in the cup. Since the cup is closed, this can be linked to a person's unconscious mind that is often shut and needs to be opened with effort. One's unconscious mind carries the secrets to their wellbeing and abilities needed to succeed. However, if you fail to open it, you can never uncover these secrets. The card also tells us about the physical realm, the importance of books and research, and magnetism. Moreover, you can also interpret the significance of abstract ideas, attraction, and romance through this card.

Just like the King of Cups is believed to have Cancer as his zodiac sign, the Queen of Cups has Scorpio as hers. This woman is a symbol of power and imagination. She has creative skills and psychic abilities. On the negative side, she can be secretive, suspicious, and aloof. Just like life should be taken seriously at times, the Queen keeps hers in control and does not take it for granted.

Pisces (Feb 29 - March 20)

The final sign of the zodiac calendar, Pisces, is symbolized by a pair of fish. This sign is known for its laid-back attitude, unlike other Water signs.

Personality Traits of Pisces

While Pisces mostly adhere to their principles and strongly express their feelings, they can sometimes be moody and care less about letting out their emotions. They are empathetic by nature and do their best to keep others happy. They are selfless and ready to help others without giving a second thought. Their creative skills and imaginative thought pattern set them apart from the rest. This is why they can easily build things from scratch and innovate. However, if things don't go their way, they can become moody or desperate, affecting others around them to varying extents.

If someone hurts them more than once, the Pisces will isolate themselves and fear showing their emotions. When expressing their feelings, they are careful and try not to hurt others. This makes them one of the most thoughtful zodiac signs. At times, they will even go out of their way to place other's needs before theirs, which is why they often lack in some areas. By contrast, Pisces can be easily influenced and swayed. No matter the nature of their goals, they will employ every tactic to achieve them once they set their minds.

Pisces and Its Tarot Cards

Pisces is closely associated with the Moon and the Page of Cups cards.

The Moon

The two main qualities that the Moon stands by are idealism and subconscious thinking. It basically means that the things you see are not always real. This card delves deep into the subconscious mind of the Pisces and describes their secretive side. It illustrates a moon looking down on the earth along with a dog and a wolf (representing the Pisces' tame and wild side, respectively). Two tall towers symbolize unity, just like the pair of fishes. While the card advocates for the practical life that most of us live, it hints at a life that can be more meaningful and mystical. We simply need to find our path and take the most meaningful road to living life to the fullest.

The Page of Cups

We can see a young person holding a cup on this card, ready to make an important announcement. This symbolizes eventfulness and news. The cup depicts a fish popping out with waves in the background. It means that the individual is either blessed with or on their way to formulate a new and life-changing idea. This new perspective should be leveraged to bring a positive change in your life. This also relates to future planning and making informed decisions to lead a comfortable life. The person on the card is believed to be kind, gentle, and creative, just like the Pisces.

Chapter 15: Master the Minor Arcana with Numerology

Now that we understand the relationship between the Major Arcana and numerology, we will explore how the Minor Arcana deck is also linked. With this knowledge, you can interpret your life decisions, personality, and intuition at a deeper level. This methodical approach is believed to be effective and mostly accurate. However, since the Minor Arcana comprises numerous cards, narrowing down your readings can be overwhelming. This is where the power of numbers can help you.

Let's take a quick recap to understand the classification of the four suits of the Minor Arcana cards based on respective elemental signs.

The Four Suits of the Minor Arcana

Suit of Wands

Sign: Fire

Quality: Momentum, energy, inspiration, and enthusiasm

Your soul's movement and energy are represented by the Suit of Wands and correspond to the Fire sign. It indicates that your actions must be supervised to pursue the right direction and experience positive change. You must find your true calling to stay driven and content. You possess the flame and passion needed to achieve your dreams, yet the only hindrance is the inability to find these qualities. While these qualities can help one attain contentment, they can also destroy them if. Learn how to use your inner power to leverage them for you, not against you.

Suit of Pentacles

Sign: Earth

Quality: Physical, wealth, material, manifestation, and career

All matters related to money, materials, resources, and the physical world are hinted at by the Suit of Pentacles and the Earth sign. Just like the earth nurtures and supports the growth and livelihood of living beings, your inner strength can help you take control of the world around you. If you search deep enough, you can find the changes needed for gaining resources and fulfilling your dreams in the physical world. However, if the person is not grounded, they can become greedy and possessive, which must be avoided at all costs.

Suit of Swords

Sign: Air

Quality: Mental, truth, communication, thoughts, and intellect

The Suit of Swords symbolizes the mind and mental energy. Whether you are indecisive or unable to utilize your mind's capabilities, this suit indicates the need to consider your options and take a clear step. Just like a double-edged sword, one's mental capabilities and power can either make or break them. Learn how to use your mental power to fulfill your dreams instead of destroying yourself. Use the movement of air as an inspiration, moving unnoticed but forcefully.

Suit of Cups

Sign: Water

Quality: Emotions, intuition, creativity, and relationships

The Suit of Cups encompasses relationships, emotions, love, and passion. As the water flows in a gentle yet constant motion, your emotions can also guide your way. If you get this suit in your reading, you may be thinking with your heart instead of your head. It can also mean that the decisions you make in serious situations may not be the best, and you that must think analytically to achieve the best outcome.

This classification will help you grasp the correlation between the Minor Arcana cards and the numbers they represent.

The Minor Arcana Tarot Cards and Numerology

You can use this interdependence to memorize the meanings of the cards with ease. The Minor Arcana deck comprises 56 cards with the numbers 1 (the Ace) through 10 (each with four suits). These 40 numbered cards are divided into four suits, and the rest are labeled as Court cards.

Let's explore the numbers of the Minor Arcana and their correspondence with the four suits (Cups, Pentacles, Swords, and Wands).

One-Ace

Qualities: Opportunity, new beginnings, potential, new ideas, and birth

As mentioned, the Ace is just starting their journey and taking the first step. While they may appear hesitant and lack self-confidence, they possess the courage and ability to attain great heights at first sight. They have a fresh perspective that is difficult to find in others. If this number pops up in your Tarot card reading, it can mean that the Ace can find you before you begin the climb.

At times, Aces can intimidate with their youthful stance and raw energy. If they get a new idea with potentially life-changing prospects, they will summon their powerful energy to get the best outcome. Even if you don't yet have an idea, this number asks you to delve deeper and find your calling. Your new idea is buried deep, and you just need guidance to unravel it. You possess the potential to trigger and experience positive change with a shift in your perspective. The way you take advantage of opportunities depends on you. More important, you must take care of your ideas, as new beginnings can often overwhelm you.

Two

Qualities: Partnership, balance, duality, attraction, waiting, and choice

Characteristics like union, pairing, and tie-ups are firmly represented by number two in the Tarot deck. Whether it's a new relationship, marriage, or business partnership, you might have recently entered or will soon enter a new important affiliation. It signifies the action of two opposite forces trying hard to become one. The notions of union and harmonious existence might affect your wellbeing. However, you must be wary of the complexities that may occur because of said affiliation.

By contrast, this partnership or union can prove to be so perfect and balanced that moving on can be quite challenging. You are comfortable and advance at your own pace, hindering your progress and having you plateau. This can also affect your decision-making and paralyze your analytical skills. However, usually, this union simply implies that the new beginnings perceived with the Ace are in place and that you need more time to plan ahead. You will also face choosing between potential partners and including the most competent one on your team.

Three

Qualities: Growth, creativity, group, increase, expression, and fruitfulness

Number three also represents group work and the idea of growing together. Your ideas and plan are in motion, and you steadily move ahead. At this stage, you may have more people joining your group and working towards progress. It also refers to the emergence of new ideas that can strengthen the existing plan. Your group is taking actionable steps and celebrating your evolution. While most readings are positive, some pairings of the suit and number three can indicate different outcomes. Since the number three is chiefly associated with the concept of completion (the holy trinity and the first polygon), it can indicate some sort of attainment in your life.

Note that the number three can be tricky and produce distinct meanings based on the suit you pull out. For example, while the Three of Swords can depict misunderstanding and sadness, the Three of Cups can mean joy and celebration. These are the two ends of the spectrum, and your reading will largely depend on the element you get.

Four

Qualities: Stability, structure, manifestation, security, organization, and foundation

Number four hints that you must expand your current idea or project to keep yourself growing. Usually, the foundation has already been laid. However, hindrance or slow progress can mean that the execution could be slow or poor. This often leads to disappointments as the outcome is unforeseeable. If you get the number four in your reading, it is a sign from the universe to push and progress to achieve expected results continuously.

Basically, your inner power, skills, and hopes have already manifested themselves in the practical world, and you just have to keep growing. You will face numerous challenges and crucial decisions, most of which will pertain to the plan in progress. Even though the number four chiefly indicates peace, certain situations can trigger this force to turn into stagnation. Reflect on your work and comprehend the changes that need to be made to keep evolving. After all, you don't want the time and effort you invested in yourself to be for nothing.

Five

Qualities: Conflict, change, instability, challenge, fluctuations, and loss

Right now, you may face several uncertainties that can create fluctuations or instability in your life. Usually, the number five signifies temporary chaos and minor setbacks. However, your project, phases, and outcomes can get permanently damaged if you don't take it seriously. You must learn to deal with the uncertainties and carve your own path towards progress. Note that most people start overthinking in times of chaos, which should be avoided.

If you haven't yet faced any setback, be prepared to face one if this card pops up in your tarot reading. The hindrance or obstacles can occur in any form, whether it's tiffs with your partners, loss in your business, or personal issues that can jeopardize the bigger picture. It is also a great time to learn from the past and turn your mistakes into lessons. However, this phase is temporary. To bounce back, you must take immediate action and stay positive. Be calm and find your way out to overcome this temporary disruption.

Six

Qualities: Harmony, cooperation, communication, recovery, peace, and adjustment

Number six is rather solution-oriented and brings peace. It indicates that you have successfully dodged the temporary hardship and are making progress. You are at peace with your partner and are working harmoniously on your project or new ideas. You may also be joining forces or bringing new members into your venture. Regardless of the direction, the union will help you achieve a desirable goal, which all parties covet.

If you are in a staggering phase, the new union will help set you straight again. You will receive plenty of guidance and empathy to overcome your issues. In essence, the number six highlights a person's needs and their desire to find true companionship. No matter the suit you get, the number six will ask you to seek help. It is time to move on from conflict and implement permanent solutions. This number also indicates the need to let go of both internal and external strife. There is always light after dark and clear skies after storms.

Seven

Qualities: Knowledge, assessment, reflection, discovery, spirituality, and independence

Number seven indicates introspection and the need to dig deeper. Stop whatever you are doing and step back. Are you on the right path? Are your life and plans going as expected? Should you make any improvements? If yes, reevaluate your trajectory and change the order of execution. At this point, you are also assessing your mistakes and learning from them. This will ensure that you do not repeat them and instead use them to pursue your path.

Even though you may feel lonely, you must reexamine your condition to fulfill your pursuit. Contemplate your authentic desires and pause if you have to. Take as much time as you need, but always come back stronger. Everyone needs a break, especially after chasing their dreams relentlessly. You have worked hard and can now afford to relax for a little while. Even during a pause, you find better ways to ameliorate your life, which is still a form of progress.

Eight

Qualities: Action, mastery, accomplishment, fortitude, and courage

Once you have experienced the phase of reflection and contemplation, it is time to integrate your actions into your true pursuit. Number eight indicates courage, momentum, action, and mastery, which means you must fight and accomplish your goals. You have the courage and skills to fulfill your destiny. All you need is some motivation and positivity, which number eight brings to the table. Furthermore, it states you are close to success and can almost taste it. You just have to cover the extra mile to make it happen.

The eight also indicates completion and achievement. You have already tasted success or are on the verge of experiencing it. It does not always mean fame, worldly success, or monetary rewards. Sometimes, it refers to the person's emotional wellbeing. In the end, you are bound to keep growing and experience a successful outcome. You may not see or feel it coming, and you may get the opportunity when you least expect it.

Nine

Qualities: Attainment, fruition, fulfillment, self-knowledge, and awakening

As you near completion, you are steadily transitioning into a stagnant or stable phase. Most individuals confuse this phase with reaching the finish line, whereas it is merely a transition in reality. You feel you have successfully completed your project, but you are not there yet. You are simply changing and evolving to be prepared for success. In a way, the contemplation and momentum the number eight inspire are slowly turning into progress, guided by the number nine.

In certain astrological readings, nine is indicated as a state of completion in place of the number ten. At this stage, you can clearly see the bigger picture and are close to the finish line. In fact, you can see it and are rapidly moving towards it. However, if you are tired and need to pause, consider taking a break to relax. You are close to the end, and it will eventually arrive. Use this time to gain knowledge, work on yourself, and foster self-awareness.

Ten

Qualities: End of a cycle, completion, renewal, or endings

By now, you have attained completion and reached the end of the cycle. Whether it's a worldly project or your emotional progress, you have successfully culminated on top. Most individuals at this point are content, both emotionally and spiritually. If you get this number in your tarot reading, you have most likely completed the circle.

As time passes, you will start the process and do it all over again. You can build a project that is completely different from the one you lived in the past. However, it is necessary to rest before you take the new path to avoid draining your energy.

To get an accurate tarot reading, combine the qualities of the numbers with the Minor Arcana card traits that show up in your spread. For example, if you get the Four of Pentacles, relate the number four to stability and the suit of Pentacles to finances. You are therefore blessed with financial stability. Similarly, the Five of Cups can mean a downfall or strife in your relationship because the number Five signifies conflict, and the suit of Cups depicts relationships and love.

Chapter 16: Understand the Major Arcana with Numerology

In its true essence, the tarot is much more than a set of cards. Although it may seem like a parlor trick clouded in magic and mystery, tarot can help you dive deep into the realms of human consciousness and recognize past and present patterns, along with your probable future. As we've seen, the tarot is divided into two different arcanas. The major arcana reveals and sheds light on the intricate aspects of your life experience using numerology, symbolism, and elements.

Most tarot enthusiasts begin by understanding the meanings associated with the major arcana cards. The major arcana correspondences can be an effective way to learn the meanings of each card. Once you grasp the key traits associated with each major arcana card, you can learn more about them in-depth. You can learn major arcana astrology, major arcana numerology, major arcana elements, and more, depending on the technique you use to read tarot cards.

This chapter will focus on the major arcana meanings hidden in the 22 tarot cards. Each card symbolizes a different experience of your psyche that ultimately leads you to understand the universal subconscious. The tribulations and trials that the major arcana cards entail can inspire and unsettle the reader. It goes without saying that the numerical figures, characters, and glyphs connected with the major arcana cards can be overwhelming for novices. This is why it's best to approach tarot as a story that depicts the Fool as the central character.

The Story of the Major Arcana Cards

The Fool (Number 0)

The story begins with the zero, the carefree Fool, unfolding the mysteries of the major arcana as he advances through the journey, unaware of what lies ahead. The Fool appears in the tarot deck wearing a white tunic and holding a flower in his hand. He is often depicted as standing at the edge of a precipice. You might see him as unaware or dim, but you'll be surprised when you understand his personality and actions. In tarot, the Fool resembles the power of the present moment. The dominant theme of the Fool card is mastering life's journey. Besides his political prowess, the Fool excels at directing others and can accumulate great wealth. He is fearless, open, and innocent, which makes this adventurous journey of self-discovery possible.

The Magician (Number 1)

When the Fool sets on his journey, the first person he encounters is the Magician, representing pure masculine energy and leadership. The Magician, being number 1, is a natural leader, unique, assertive, yet often stubborn. This tarot card represents intellectual development, problem-solving skills, independence, and endless creativity. The Magician is highly inventive, impulsive, and entrepreneurial. He has a conscious mind and pioneering instincts. This card symbolizes a strong willingness to assert personal views out in the world and the ability to harness one's talents towards the betterment of self.

The High Priestess (Number 2)

Next, the Fool encounters the High Priestess, sitting patiently in front of Solomon's temple. Known as the guardian of the secrets of divine power, the High Priestess embodies pure feminine energy, equilibrium, and immense knowledge. The mysterious, powerful, and magical forces of intuition are embodied in the High Priestess. These intangible forces enable her to explore the realms of magic. She may struggle with decision-making and self-confidence and is often oversensitive. This card in tarot represents mild and peaceful energy. The High Priestess is socially aware, loves balance, and is an excellent peacemaker.

The Empress (Number 3)

The Empress is considered the earthly counterpart of the feminine High Priestess. Like the number 3, she represents communication, divine feminine bonding, and harmony. As the mother of the Fool, she is known to be nurturing, loving, and kind-spirited. She represents abundance, fun, and optimism. Known to be a natural entertainer and a skilled orator, the Empress is expressive and can easily strike conversations. Sometimes, she suffers from extreme self-indulgence, craves opportunities, and may lack focus. However, the Empress finds solace in her vivid imagination, creativity, and unwavering optimism.

The Emperor (Number 4)

The Emperor is the earthly embodiment of the masculine Magician and the Fool's father. This tarot card represents law and order. The Emperor is hardworking, focused, and disciplined by nature. To protect his realm and the softness of the Empress, he builds walls and creates firm boundaries from the external world. The Emperor is a creative builder who thrives on planning and systematic approaches. Known to be very practical and a natural supervisor, the Emperor shares his knowledge with the young Fool to help him find security and establish boundaries.

The Hierophant (Number 5)

The young Fool leaves the safety of his home, empowered by the knowledge of his parents. When he starts exploring the structured world, the Fool encounters the Hierophant. This card symbolizes freedom and adventure. The Hierophant is known to have a restless mind that questions everything and learns from experiences. This impulsive spirit dislikes monotony and thrives on constant change. In addition, the Hierophant is blessed with great sex appeal and loves physical indulgence that involves all human senses.

The Lovers (Number 6)

As the Fool continues on his journey, he meets the Lovers. The Lovers card represents responsibility, beauty, honesty, harmony, generosity, and symmetry in tarot. From them, he realizes the power of choice and that his own doings will shape his future. The Lovers card also symbolizes protectiveness, fairness, peace, and love. The number 6 is associated with discernment, protectiveness, and intolerance of hostility. In short, for the lovers, the heart is where the home is. The Lovers are known to prefer a domestic life and are community dwellers. They crave love and attention, are naturally artistic, and love attractive surroundings.

The Chariot (Number 7)

Educated by the Lovers, the Fool is now ready to apply his knowledge to the real world. To embark on this adventure, however, he must pass the Chariot. It represents graduation, a sign that the Fool has sufficient knowledge to face real-world challenges. In tarot, the Chariot card is associated with the mind. It represents dreams, philosophy, and intuition. The number 7 is sacred and represents spirituality and deep thinking. The Chariot is anti-social and a natural loner who prefers isolation. It is contemplative, analytical, and studious. However, the chariot's excellent mental powers enable it to appreciate details.

The Strength (Number 8)

After graduating, the Fool faces his first challenge in the form of Strength. The Strength card in the tarot represents materialism. In parallel, the number 8 is associated with wealth and abundance. The Strength card also embodies ideals of stability, safety, and security. This card is associated with leadership, financial balance, spiritual growth, and courage. A balance between spiritual and mental is what keeps this card satisfied. This card represents large reserves of strength and energy. It is also known to have exceptional organizational skills capable of managing large businesses.

The Hermit (Number 9)

Tested by the challenges of Strength, the Fool finds himself spiraling into the world of the Hermit. Finding himself alone with his thoughts, the Fool learns about introspection. The Hermit card represents wisdom and is known as a universalist. The number 9 is associated with compassion and innate wisdom. The Hermit is blessed with abstract thinking and formidable energy. Often viewed as naive, the Hermit must share wisdom with others and learn to say no. Known as a humanitarian, he is idealistic, merciful, and tolerant.

The Wheel of Fortune (Number 10)

Once detached from the outer world, the Fool understands that life is a game to be played and a set of riddles waiting to be solved. These twists and turns are a result of fate and choices. This is when the Wheel of Fortune appears as if a manifestation of the Fool's newly found knowledge. This card in tarot represents new beginnings. The number 10 in numerology is associated with influence, opinion, and spirituality. The Wheel of Fortune is a clear thinker and possesses great pragmatism and leadership skills. It represents the change in fortune, connection with consciousness, and a new cycle of energy.

Justice (Number 11)

As the Fool gets accustomed to the ever-changing nature of fortune, he is led to the Justice card. Here, he learns how decisions are made and implemented. The Justice card represents a master's intuitive visionary. In numerology, the number 11 is called a master number and is associated with enlightenment. The Justice card is idealistic, naturally perceptive, and quite creative. It draws energy from cosmic forces and is a natural educator. It has a keen sense of justice and a great curiosity for the metaphysical. The Justice card is a natural catalyst, has boundless creative potential, and is known to be positively decisive.

The Hanged Man (Number 12)

The Fool soon learns that life is not so black and white when he encounters the Hanged Man. He finds himself between two worlds, trying to adopt a fresher perspective. In tarot, the Hanged Man card symbolizes the law of reversal. It also represents a period of waiting or suspended decision-making. The Hanged Man observes the world from a different perspective, can look beneath the surface, and believes that reality is an illusion. He is the epitome of wisdom and has tremendous inner strength. Known to be deeply serene, the Hanged Man is spiritual, analytical, and can tolerate diverse beliefs. The number 12 is associated with the importance of natural and universal laws.

Death (Number 13)

His uncomfortable encounter with the Hanged Man makes the Fool realize that whatever he accepted as blind truth was the ideology of his former tutors. This is when the Death card appears to release him from the Emperor's teachings, Empress, Hierophant, Lovers, Justice, and every other notion accumulated since childhood. In tarot, the Death card represents karmic rebirth. It suggests constant change, destruction, and reconstruction. This card is all about regeneration and transformation. The number 13 is associated with psychic abilities, transmutation of energy, and limitless creativity. The Death card also symbolizes "all-or-nothing" energy.

Temperance (Number 14)

The experience with Death changes the Fool forever. His understanding takes the form of Temperance. The angel of the Temperance card provides the Food with a deeper understanding of spirituality. The Fool finds his emotion stabilized and the extremities of life connected through a middle path. In tarot, the Temperance card represents moderation. The number 14 is associated with vivid sexual energy and imagination. The Temperance loves adrenaline and excitement. It learns by experience and loves a fast and furious life. Temperance needs to beware of extremes and learn about caution and the importance of slowing down every now and then

The Devil (Number 15)

The clarity that comes with the Temperance reveals the blind spots of the Fool. These hidden spots take the form of the Devil. With the Devil's appearance, the Fool's subconscious urges manifest themselves in the form of attachment and addiction. The Devil card represents discernment and circumstantial bondage. It is naturally magnetic and strong-willed. The number 15 is associated with ambition, perseverance and also symbolizes responsibility. It is largely associated with the home and family.

The Tower (Number 16)

The amount of stress, manipulation, and tension that arises due to the Devil are short-lived. The awe and shock of the Tower awaken the Fool. The Tower card resonates with the notion of awakening. It displays an expressive, perceptive, and often forceful personality. The Tower may face challenges such as material losses due to emotional issues, temporary setbacks, destructive temper, and impatience. It can easily assess circumstances and is blessed with clear-sighted intellect.

The Star (Number 17)

The Fool's inner world walls are shattered by a lightning bolt from the heavens, allowing the Star to be reborn. Perhaps one of the most hopeful and magical moments of the Fool's life, the Star's divine assistance blesses him with new and healthy ideas. In tarot, the Star card represents success. It symbolizes the desire for truth, determination, and insightfulness. The Star's auspicious vibrations and fine thinking help the Fool find wise ways in the material world. The Star is often associated with executive leadership abilities, high focus, and the Aquarian influence.

The Moon (Number 18)

The level of transcendence that the Fool finds with the Star has a dark side. From the shadows, the Moon appears. It reminds the Fool of the cycle of women and the tides of the ocean. The psychic and profound Moon embodies all that is mysterious and uncontrollable. The Moon represents shadow development in tarot and is associated with natural healing ability, intense emotions, imagination, and sensitivity. This card is also associated with emotional instability, inexperienced energy, anxiety, and nervousness. The Moon is intuitive, receptive, highly influenced by the subconscious, and can develop high focus.

The Sun (Number 19)

As the Moon starts to set, the Fool can feel his journey ending. His feelings are confirmed as the Sun rises with the promise of returning home. The Sun card epitomizes independence in tarot and is perceived as an excellent speaker and a gifted leader. The card is associated with high intellect, art, and science. The Sun must master emotions, control impulsiveness, and restrain from self-pity. The card is the sign of life and light. The Sun is blessed with divine guiding power.

Judgment (Number 20)

As the Fool returns to his ancestral castle, he is ready to reveal everything he learned throughout the journey. This is where the Judgment card is revealed. In tarot, the Judgment card represents cooperation, collaboration, and decisions. This card is the power behind the throne and is naturally diplomatic. One must learn to master emotions, adapt to diverse perceptions, and distinguish between what is true and false.

The World (Number 21)

Eventually, the Fool ends his journey as the final inner works are completed. The World welcomes the Fool. While it represents the end of one's journey, the World hints at the start of another adventure. The endless cycle of life is perhaps the deepest level of wisdom that the Fool learns from his journey of self-discovery. The World card, in tarot, represents cyclical integration and is associated with a positive attitude, freedom, and liberation. The number 21 is a fortunate number that represents a positive outlook on life. It symbolizes the union of love and wisdom. The World can often be greedy or selfish. However, it is just another opportunity for the Fool to discover new ways of learning and growing.

Chapter 17: The Major Arcana and the Planets

In tarot, every astrological sign corresponds to a major arcana card. Throughout this chapter, we will discuss the ten major arcana cards ruled by planets and how these cards embody the characteristics of the astrological signs. This chapter will also help you gain insights into your Sun, Moon, and Rising sign using tarot. By the end, you must gather valuable knowledge that will help you outline your personality using the connection between astrology and tarot.

In astrology, the signs and meanings associated with the planets originate in Roman and Greek mythology. These correspondences are a great tool for learning about the key traits and notions associated with each planet and zodiac. Knowledge of the planets can be used in tarot reading. If you are new to tarot, this chapter will enable you to grasp the connection between the planets and the major arcana cards.

Major Arcana Cards and Corresponding Planets

The Sun

The Sun symbolizes conscience, fame, identity, individuality, life, positivity, success, and victory. The positioning of the Sun, and the zodiac signs at the time of your birth, determine your Sun sign. In tarot, the Sun card represents happiness, success, and recognition. It is believed to be a good omen and a form of divination. The Sun card helps predict the positive things, success and achievements, which will come to you in the future. The Sun symbolizes good health and positivity.

The High Priestess - The Moon

The Moon corresponds to the High Priestess. The Moon is traditionally associated with femininity, dreams, and creativity. In many cultures, the Moon symbolizes feelings, emotions, reputation, psychic abilities, and the human subconscious. In tarot, the High Priestess card is associated with emotions and psychic ability. While the card represents intuition, it also symbolizes cheating and secrets. You'll find that the High Priestess is connected with darkness and night, not unlike the Moon. This is why they are often associated with occult abilities, infidelity, and hidden information. Since the Moon is visible at night, it is mostly connected to dreaming, creativity, and imagination. The Moon also symbolizes crabs, oceans, and water.

The Magician - Mercury

The planet Mercury corresponds to the Magician card. The Magician represents diplomacy, enterprise, and knowledge. As a good and witty orator, the Magician excels at communication. This ability to speak logically and thoughtfully can make the Magician a good showman and a good conman. In Greek mythology, Mercury is believed to be the god of thieves and symbolizes social networking and communication. The key traits associated with Mercury are knowledge, networking, and travel. The planet Mercury is known as the planetary ruler of the rising sign and symbolizes how you connect with others.

The Empress - Venus

The planet Venus corresponds to the Empress card. Venus is one of the most beloved Greek goddesses. She is worshipped as the goddess of love. In mythology, Venus's symbols include girdle, Myrtle, rose, and shell. Venus represents love, relationships, and romance. In astrology, Venus represents beauty, desire, fertility, harmony, love, and sexuality.

Interestingly, the Empress in the tarot represents harmony and fertility, just like Venus. The Empress card usually predicts the start of a new relationship, pregnancy, and is associated with children's birth. Venus appears in the form of the Empress in tarot, and it is a card that represents balance.

The Tower - Mars

Mars appears as the Tower card. It is known as the planet of aggression, anger, determination, drive, masculinity, war, and will. Mars corresponds to the Tower in tarot and represents destruction, negativity, and ruins. Although Mars has some positive attributes, they are often read quite negatively. Swords, shields, and spears are symbols of Mars. Dreaming of these things can be signs of future conflicts, troubles, or arguments. Mars can be used to reflect your level of aggression, how brave you are, and how quickly you can sort out your problems.

The Wheel of Fortune - Jupiter

The planet Jupiter corresponds to the Wheel of Fortune card. Jupiter is believed to be the planet of luck. If the planet appears to be well placed in someone's chart, it means they are naturally fortunate and blessed with good things. However, it doesn't mean they will find them effortlessly. Instead, they will be nudged in the right direction by the universe. Just like Jupiter, the Wheel of Fortune is associated with fortune and luck. The card also symbolizes confidence, charity, and expansion. The planet Jupiter, just like the Wheel of Fortune, represents leadership, authority, and power. Besides the prediction of luck, Jupiter can also help reveal destiny and fate.

The World - Saturn

The planet Saturn appears as the World. Saturn corresponds to the World card and represents limitations, restrictions, and responsibility. In mythology, Saturn represents the things that must be done, whether you feel like doing them or not. Traditionally, Saturn symbolizes authority, a sense of duty, and responsibility. Helped by Saturn, you can reveal your shortcomings, whether you are truly content with where you are in life. It can also highlight the responsibilities you have that you shun away. Similar to Saturn, the World card represents a significant change in your life when starting a new phase and leaving the old one behind.

The Fool - Uranus

The planet Uranus corresponds to the Fool. Uranus is associated with change, individuality, originality, and technology. The planet Uranus represents the beginning of the age of technology and the industrial revolution. In tarot, the Fool advises others to implement change in their lives. The Fool is depicted as someone who is airy and difficult to pin down. The Fool card tells you that you don't want to be shackled to something forever. Just like the Fool, the planet Uranus showcases a dislike for responsibility and someone who finds joy in doing their own thing.

The Hanged Man - Neptune

The planet Neptune symbolizes dreams, intuition, and spirituality. In tarot, Neptune corresponds to the Hanged Man card. If Neptune is well placed on someone's chart, it means they have the power of prophecy and deep psychic abilities. However,

Neptune can also represent clarity. Although it is primarily associated with positive qualities, if Neptune is badly placed in someone's chart, it can mean that the person may face difficulty in making decisions. The Hanged Man card represents spiritual awakening, dreams, and intuition, just like the planet Neptune. Like Neptune, this card symbolizes uncertainty and a poor sense of orientation.

Judgment - Pluto

The planet Pluto is known as the planet of change, renewal, rebirth, and transformation. In Roman mythology, Pluto was believed to incarnate Roma, god of death, which is fitting since death is the bringer of renewal and rebirth. Since Pluto was only discovered recently, it represents new beginnings and major life changes ahead. In tarot, Pluto is believed to rule the Judgment card. They both represent life-changing opportunities and intense transformation.

Understanding the Sun, Moon, and Rising Signs

In astrology, the zodiac signs along with celestial bodies communicate a unique signature, known as a birth chart. This unique cosmic signature is a map that reveals the positions of the planets, the sun, the moon, and the stars at the time and place of birth. The Sun, Moon, and Rising signs are the three primary planetary points that reveal your everyday personality. Another interesting thing to note is that each astrological sign corresponds to a major arcana card in tarot. This section will discuss what your Sun, Moon, and Rising signs say about you and which major arcana cards correspond to the astrological signs. Are you ready for this intentional journey of self-exploration? Without further ado, let's begin by understanding the Sun, Moon, and Rising signs.

Sun Sign

Almost everybody knows their Sun sign as this is the most discussed aspect in astrology. The Sun sign can be found within a specific zodiac in your birth chart. It speaks of your identity and how you express yourself. It represents the powerful energy that urges you to seek your true self and express it in the best possible way. It also represents the way you express your individuality and how you portray yourself to the world. In other words, your Sun sign is who you are at your core.

Rejuvenating your energy, socializing, and involving yourself with people can prove very useful. If your Sun sign is Cancer, Pisces, or Scorpio, you will experience deep motivation through emotional desires and feel recharged by being meditative and mindful. If your Sun sign is Capricorn, Taurus, or Virgo, you will feel recharged by being productive and engaging with the physical world to stimulate your senses. These signs are very practical in life and are deeply motivated by materialistic needs. If your Sun sign is Sagittarius, Leo, or Aries, you feel recharged by pursuing your ambitions and through physical activity. Your aspirations and goals keep you highly inspired. Last, if your Sun sign is Aquarius, Gemini, or Libra, the best way to recharge is to socialize and express yourself intellectually.

Moon Sign

Your Moon sign reveals everything that you feel. It is associated with your inner emotional self and how you deal with your feelings. The Moon sign also represents your intuition, subconscious, and spirituality. This aspect of your life is generally hidden from the outside world and may be evident only to you and those closest to you. It can be understood as your subconscious side that drives your emotional reactions. This sign can help you understand how to recharge and nurture your emotions healthily. It helps you feel the emotions of joy, pleasure, sorrow, and pain.

If the Moon in your birth chart is positioned in Cancer, Pisces, or Scorpio, you will feel in alignment with the universe and your inner self while experiencing deep emotions. These signs are sensitive to changes and may emotionally react when going through change. If your Moon sign is Sagittarius, Leo, or Aries, you will feel the most aligned with yourself when doing something with confidence. Showing strength and refraining from self-doubt can be satisfying for these signs. Experiencing a change in life can be exciting for you and motivate you to act. If your Moon sign is Capricorn, Virgo, or Taurus, being productive and getting closer to goals can make you feel the most aligned with your inner self. These signs react to changing circumstances with stability and steadiness. If your Moon sign is Aquarius, Gemini, or Libra, you are most in alignment with your inner self when you interact with others and express your ideas. These signs react to change with proper evaluation and discernment.

Rising Sign

Last but not least, the Rising sign is the sign that was present on the eastern horizon at the time of your birth. Also known as the ascendant sign, it reveals how you reflect and project on the outside world. This is how you appear to other people and how the outer world perceives you. Your Rising sign can be understood as your apparent style and social personality. It represents your inner and your outer world.

If you have Cancer, Pieces, or Scorpio as your Rising sign, you make many decisions based on your emotions and are easily influenced by your environment. It is common for people with these signs to be empathetic and sensitive. If your Rising sign is Aries, Sagittarius, or Leo, you possess great energy and vitality. You are confident, goal-oriented, yet often too blunt. Having Capricorn, Virgo, or Taurus as your Rising sign means you are factual and have a steadfast approach to life. Finally, if your Rising sign is Aquarius,

Gemini, or Libra, you are friendly, inquisitive, and verbally expressive.

Major Arcana Correspondences of the Sun, Moon, and Rising Signs

Now that we understand the meanings associated with the astrological signs and discovered your three big signs (the Sun, Moon, and Rising), it's time to apply this knowledge to tarot and discover more about yourself in depth. In this section, you will learn about the tarot cards corresponding to the zodiac signs. Each astrological sign has a corresponding major arcana card. For each of your Sun, Moon, and Rising signs, you will be able to find the tarot cards associated with them and better understand what your cosmic signature says about you.

Aries - The Emperor

Like the authoritative Emperor, Aries represents a fierce leader, impulsive yet balanced. Both the Emperor and Aries tend to be independent but are embracing at the same time.

Aquarius - The Star

Aquarius shares the eccentricity of the Star. The creative and innovative Aquarius is capable of forward-thinking. Their aspiration inspires others. Spiritual exploration comes naturally to the Star and Aquarius.

Cancer - The Chariot

Cancer corresponds to the Chariot. Like the Chariot's forward motion, Cancer represents the willpower to keep moving in the right direction. The Chariot and Cancer symbolize control, emotions, and victory.

Capricorn - The Devil

The hardworking Capricorn is paired up with the Devil. Capricorns can be willful and work hard to achieve their goals. However, they are prone to becoming workaholics, giving in to worldly temptations or other addictions.

Gemini - The Lovers

The dynamic Gemini love to follow their passion, just like the Lovers. Gemini, like the Lovers card, represents exploration and self-love.

Leo - Strength

The powerful and commanding Leo corresponds to the Strength card. This card symbolizes taking control over your power and strength. Both represent exuberance and immense strength, which must be tamed and controlled.

Libra - Justice

Just like the Justice card, Libra represents maintaining balance, encouraging fairness, and being decisive. Both symbolize healthy communication.

Pisces - The Moon

Pieces correspond to the Moon card in the tarot. Given the deep and imaginative nature of Pisces, it pairs well with the mysterious and intimidating Moon. The key quality of both Pieces and the Moon is to listen to one's intuition.

Sagittarius - Temperance

The patient and moderate Temperance card is paired with the fair and open-minded Sagittarius. The Temperance card, just like Sagittarius, displays generosity, sincerity, and friendliness.

Scorpio - Death

Scorpio corresponds to the Death card. Their shared qualities represent endings, transitions, and cycles. They welcome change and not afraid to replace things with new ones.

Taurus - The Hierophant

The grounded and patient Taurus corresponds to the Hierophant card. This card symbolizes conformity, institution, and tradition. Mentorship is a key quality that links Taurus and the Hierophant.

Virgo - The Hermit

The practical Virgo is paired with the Hermit card. Deep introspection is a quality found in both the Hermit and Virgo. They are creative, rarely tempted by the outside world, and content in their situation.

Chapter 18: Tarot Spreads

In simple terms, a tarot spread is defined as the number of chosen cards and the way they open before you. They reveal the answer to the question posed and give you the ability to interpret those answers. From a tarot spread, you can learn how to see current circumstances clearly, get insights about past influences and what the future might hold for you. In a way, the tarot cards will form a map to help you make the right decisions no matter what occurs or when without pointing you in a specific direction. This chapter analyzes the most common tarot card layouts, including the one-card spread, the three-card spread, the Celtic cross spread, and the zodiac spread, teaching you how to master them.

Learning the art of tarot reading by yourself will bring you immense benefits, as it is free and only requires a little practice. First, you will need to understand the meaning of the different Major and Minor Arcana cards. Then, look at the cards and hold them in your hand as often as you have a chance. The more you use and handle your deck of cards, the more you charge them with your own energy, making your readings more specific and reliable. Once you grasp their essence, with some creativity, you can form any tarot spread. Consulting the subject of your interest will create the right atmosphere only for the reading, which will enable you to connect with your energy. Burning some incense, lighting up a few candles, or even playing soft music are all superb, effective ways to set the mood for a tarot reading. Whether you are a beginner or an advanced reader, these methods can help you open your mind and spread your energy outwards.

The One-Card Spread

One-card tarot spreads are ideal for simple, quick readings. It allows you to connect to each card more deeply by doing only a few short readings a day. If you need an answer to a specific question or some general guidance for the day ahead, one card may be all you need to help you out. This is also the best way to introduce novices to this type of fortune-telling.

To begin, take your deck of cards and choose one of the 22 Major Arcana cards randomly. Without looking at it, leave the card facing down at the beginning of the day, and turn it over at the end of it. Reflect on your day, linking your experiences to the card you drew. Try to remember this match and your mood for future readings. It is recommended to repeat this practice for 22 days and then repeat it for the same duration while also trying to guess the card you have drawn.

Once you have learned how to match your experiences with each card, you will be ready to ask some questions from your cards. Remember, start with a question that requires a simple "yes" or "no" for an answer, after which you can transition towards more complex ones. Advanced spreads can take quite some time to master, but once you practice the one-card pull long enough, complicated spreads will be easier to master. It is vital to clear your mind for a more accurate reading and only then begin to shuffle your deck. While you shuffle the cards, think of the question you seek an answer to. Choose any Major Arcana card whose back catches your attention and try to interpret it. If the card you have chosen is the World, the Sun, the Magician, the Temperance, the

Strength, the Star, or the Chariot, then the answer to your question is "yes." By contrast, drawing the Devil, the Hanged Man, the Hermit, the Tower, and the Moon, will signify "no." If the card that came up is the Lovers or the Wheel of Fortune, your question doesn't have an answer, as these two represent indecision. Try formulating the question differently or seeking an answer again later in the day. With practice, you can determine a card for each day of the week, month and year.

In your reading, you may inquire as to the experience that awaits you on that day. If you have a challenging day ahead of you, a one-card spread can show you what strengths you muster to help you out. You can use any occurrence to help yourself and others. This is a good way to learn what you are being called to share or express each day, as it can strengthen your communication with others. It can also help boost your confidence by discovering which part of you needs more acceptance and love and where you are on your healing journey.

The Three-Card Spread

Like the one-card spread, the three-card tarot is also ideal for simple questions, although it is less beginner-friendly. Since you will need to select three cards from the deck and assign three meanings to them, you should already be familiar with what the cards represent. The most practical way to interpret those three cards is by considering them an answer related to your present, past, and future. When you select your cards from the deck, lay them face down with the future card placed in the middle, as this one is heavily affected by the other two. The card on your left should be your past card, and the one on the right should signify the present. Always begin your reading with your past experience and finish it with future answers.

Your Past

Your past card can grant you the opportunity to reflect on your past and discover anything that may be holding you back from realizing your full potential. Sometimes, we are confronted with intense emotions or lessons we don't take time to examine closely. Whether it happened a week or a year prior, there could be something keeping you unsettled. In fact, your past has a significant influence on your energy, and you will need to resolve it before you can successfully move forward. This is precisely why you must begin your reading with your past card. Only after leaving behind your past ordeals can you focus on your present and, most importantly, on your future. It is best to concentrate more on your experience the week leading up to the session for a more accurate reading.

Your Present

After laying your foundation by understanding the past, you can now turn over your present card. With this card, you will be able to evaluate your current situation and mood, which can also give you valuable insights into your mental health. While the past might be affecting your present, the solution for older problems is often found in present times. For example, you may have a deep, unfulfilled desire you were not even aware of until you got in touch with your inner emotions. Whatever caused you to feel exhausted can now be resolved by resting. The first part of your resolution will be revealed to you through your present card, which will show you how to start your journey. The solution is probably already there in your subconscious, waiting to be discovered. Here, make sure to direct your energy towards only a couple of days after the reading.

Your Future

The last card you drew indicates your future. Most specifically, it can shift your focus on an event that may happen the week after the reading. After identifying your problem and its solution from the previous cards, the future card can show you how to achieve it. Overcoming traumas and other negative emotions is only possible once you can identify the right things. When we work towards a certain goal, we often focus on the things we cannot do well rather than the ones we can. By showing you what served you until then, the future card can prevent you from wasting time finding the actions needed to carry on. If you put more effort into taking the most effective steps only, you will be more likely to succeed. However, these steps will be useful only if you consider the first two cards carefully and interpret them correctly. Otherwise, your future may turn out to be different, despite what its corresponding card holds.

The Celtic Cross Spread

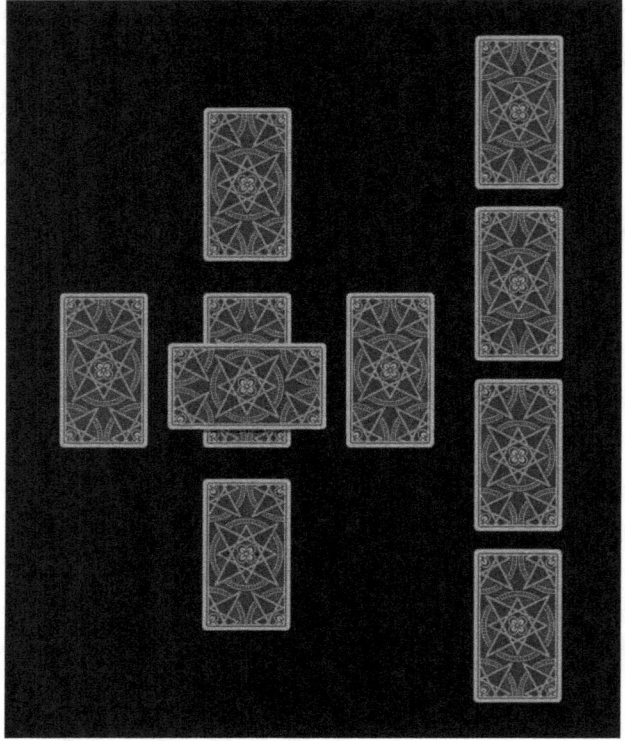

Celtic Cross Spread

After practicing basic tarot spreads, you will also learn how to perform more advanced readings, such as Celtic cross spreads. Since it provides you with detailed analysis and interpretation techniques, its main purpose is to answer a specific question. More often than not, our emotions stem from several issues. Celtic cross spreads use ten cards from your deck, and by reading them one by one, you can interpret and focus on one problem and solution at a time.

Place your first card vertically on the middle of the table and put the second one on top of it horizontally. The next four numbers should be placed around the first two and be read clockwise. Cards number 7-10 should be placed in descending order, on the right to the rest of the cards. Arranging the cards in a face-down position and revealing them as you proceed can be helpful if you are learning this spread. However, you will soon learn that placing them all facing up from the beginning can be just as efficient.

Interpreting the Cards in the Celtic Cross Spread

1. **The Person in Question**: Usually, this is the person who seeks answers and is being read for. If this person cannot relate to the meaning of the cards, the answer may have been meant for someone close to them, like a friend or relative.

2. **A Potential Situation**: This card reveals meaningful circumstances in a person's life, whether or not it is related to the question they have asked. In any case, a challenge or obstacle will turn up, along with a possible solution.

4. **The Basic Foundation**: Related to the potential situation and is often a possible event from a distant past. This influence helps determine the main problem and the resolution.

5. **A Recent Event:** While it generally represents the influence of the near past, this card might have links to the previous one. The current problem may be caused by an old trauma or be completely unrelated.

6. **The Near Future**: This card shows how the potential situation will evolve in the next few weeks or months. It can also reveal a totally unrelated event and bear great significance for the person inquiring.

7. **The Present Problem:** If you would like to know whether the situation is about to be resolved, this card can help you figure it out. Whether the expected outcome is

positive or negative, you will see where you stand in the present.

8. **Other Influences:** This card reveals how the people you surround yourself with influence your situation. Their energy can have an impact on the possible outcome of your issue. However, knowing this can help you take back control.

9. **Internal Resolution:** Because your emotions have an enormous impact on your actions, revealing them might help you find a resolution sooner. Here, you will see if there is any conflict between your conscious and subconscious desires.

10. **Conflicted Emotions:** Whether or not they are deep-rooted, your fears and hopes can be conflicted, preventing you from finding an efficient solution to your problem. You may hope for one outcome and dread it at the same time.

11. **Possible Outcome**: After analyzing all other cards, this last one may present the final piece of the puzzle. If you interpreted the previous cards correctly, this one should show you a long-term solution, extending as far as a year in the future.

The Zodiac Spread

The Zodiac Spread

If you have little experience with simple tarot layouts but aren't ready to try a Celtic Cross spread yet, consider exploring the Zodiac spread. Despite using 12 cards, this spread is easier to comprehend than the previous one. It's generally an excellent spread to use for holistic readings when you have more deep-rooted questions to explore. Given that the Zodiac spread provides answers for general, albeit important, questions, this reading is best conducted on occasions when you find yourself at a crossroads in your life.

While there are many ways to perform and interpret a Zodiac layout reading, most use twelve cards, each representing a house of the zodiac map. After clearing your mind, infuse your energy into the cards while shuffling them, and you should visualize your question. Lay the first card on your left, at the 9 o'clock position, and follow with the rest going counterclockwise until you reach a full circle. Occasionally, a 13th card is added to the middle of the spread. However, this can make the reading slightly more complicated. So, if you are new at this, it is recommended that you start with the 12-card layout.

The 12 houses of the Zodiac tarot spread are as follow:

1. **The First House:** This house represents your state of being and general outlook on life. Besides showing you how other people see you, including your physical appearance, this card can also give you insights into how you view yourself.

2. **The Second House:** This card shows your rapport to your professional life and self-worth and can help you set your priorities more clearly. It can also reveal if you have a hidden potential you can explore to earn more money.

12. **The Third House:** This house can help you explore your general surroundings, such as your workplace or social settings. Additionally, it covers your relationships with people you meet daily but who aren't close to emotionally.

13. **The Fourth House:** This house shows your connection with the people close to you. Your partner, children, or parents will show up here, as will the stability of your relationship with them.

14. **The Fifth House:** The house of your creativity reveals what you enjoy in life. It also shows how you use your creative side to resolve problematic situations that arise in your life.

15. **The Sixth House:** This card can highlight negative areas in your health and indicate the need for change. Whether you need to pay attention to healthier nutrition, better rest, or personal hygiene, you can find the answer here.

16. **The Seventh House:** This is a house of partnership, both legal and personal. It can be used to find a suitable partner, whether for a romantic interest, in business, or just a friendship.

17. **The Eighth House:** This is the card that reveals all your secrets. Everything will show up here from the grief about your family members passing away or something unexpected you would rather not talk about.

18. **The Ninth House:** This card can reveal your true potential and all the ways you can grow as a human. It covers things like how you can earn more money, but it can help realize other dreams, such as traveling.

19. **The Tenth House:** Like the previous card, this house also helps you realize your full potential, only in more professional settings. It can show you what career goals you should set for yourself and the kind of public image you should display.

20. **The Eleventh House:** This is the house of generosity towards the people in your life. It focuses on showing you how much empathy you have toward others and how they see you as a result.

21. **The Twelfth House:** All negative emotions you haven't dealt with (but that still lurk in your subconscious) will be revealed in this house. The card also shows how these thoughts limit you from being the best version of yourself.

Conclusion

As you know by now, astrology is a fascinating subject that holds the power to change a person's life. The position of the stars and alignment with certain planets highlight an individual's life, personality, wellbeing, inner thoughts, and intuition. Astrology implies that an individual is attuned to the universe and survives in harmony. Now that you have learned everything about Astrology and its implications in zodiac signs, tarot, planets, and numerology, it is time to experience the effects and bring positive change in your life.

To wrap up, let's briefly look at the subjects we covered throughout the book and apply them to begin seeing positive changes.

Planets and their respective signs play a significant role in our lives by unraveling our true personalities and guiding us on the path towards enlightenment. The way the planets are positioned is expressed through Natal charts. They are also called Birth charts and reveal your hidden tendencies and desires. The ten planets in the realm of astrology are the Sun, the Moon, Mercury, Venus, Mars, Jupiter, Saturn, Uranus, Neptune, and Pluto. Each one represents a zodiac sign, namely Aries, Taurus, Gemini, Cancer, Leo, Virgo, Libra, Scorpio, Sagittarius, Capricorn, Aquarius, and

Pisces. These 12 zodiac signs are further divided into four elemental groups, i.e., Earth, Fire, Water, and Air.

Sun Sign Astrology takes the position of the sun into account when determining a person's sign. The location of the zodiac sign is deciphered to find their sun sign. The twelve zodiac signs mentioned above are divided into specific months based on the sun's position. Each of the zodiac signs has distinct ruling planets as well. Furthermore, each sun sign falls under a part of every season, which are labeled as modalities. Regardless of the season or time of the year, certain zodiac signs share similar traits as they fall under the same modality. These Sun signs also display four personality type variants: sanguine, choleric, melancholic, and phlegmatic.

Moon Sign Astrology is often disregarded because of the burden imposed by the Sun signs. However, like every celestial body that plays an important part in astrology, the moon also rules and controls some zodiac signs. The moon represents an individual's hidden intentions, deep-rooted emotions, and innermost feelings. In other words, these are the feelings that one is unable to process and express. If you feel misunderstood, your moon and sun may be failing to cooperate. The sensitive side of the zodiac signs is interpreted by the moon's energy on respective groups, which gives rise to the emotional zodiac signs.

Numerology is the study of numbers with significant values that distinctly examine the characteristics of individuals. They are also used in the world of astrology to derive new concepts and ideas. Your primary traits, thoughts, feelings, and soul's calling all point to a specific set of numbers, which are significant to your being. These are then called your "lucky" numbers. While all zodiac signs are assigned certain numbers based on collective traits, each person can have a different number that best describes their essence. You can study the numbers and compare them with your own personality based on Odd, Even, and Master numbers.

Your Personality and Heart Number can be figured out using the science of numerology and considering your personality. Refer to the table and guidelines again to discover your personality number based on your name. These numbers represent your true personality, traits, heart, and inner calling. The power of numbers is such that they can reveal your outer behavior and your heart's desire. Interpreting your personality and heart numbers will help you realize your true purpose and put you on the right path. More importantly, it will provide courage and motivate you to achieve your goals and fulfill your ultimate purpose.

Tarot card reading is the art of reading and deciphering a set of illustrated cards representing a person's true personality, hidden intentions, and life path. A standard tarot card deck contains 78 cards divided into two groups, i.e., Major Arcana and Minor Arcana cards. While the Major Arcana cards symbolize a person's personality and major traits, the Minor Arcana cards reveal their encounters and experiences in day-to-day life. This helps them understand the bigger picture while acting towards positive change incrementally. The Major Arcana set is a deck of 22 numbered cards, and the Minor Arcana set contains 56 cards divided into four suits, the Wands, Pentacles, Swords, and Cups. You can master the art of tarot card reading by practicing different spreads, different ways of laying Tarot cards, and opening them for reading.

The Four Signs and Their Tarot Cards represent respective zodiac signs and reveal hidden truths. As you learned, the four signs are Fire, Earth, Air, and Wind, and they are assigned a set of cards that closely resemble them. Each card is depicted as one of these natural elements and resonates with certain zodiac signs. You can compare and relate your zodiac sign with its tarot card to analyze your personality on a deeper level. While some Tarot cards overlap with certain zodiac signs, most of them are assigned to dedicated Major and Minor Arcana for better understanding.

Tarot and Numbers are also closely connected, and their influence is intertwined. Each Major and Minor Arcana card is dedicated to specific numbers that are placed in order. If you need to strengthen your tarot card reading practice, read and interpret the numbers to reinforce your art.

Here is a glyph dictionary reference for zodiac signs and planets for a better understanding.

Zodiac Signs

♈	Aries	♎	Libra
♉	Taurus	♏	Scorpio
♊	Gemini	♐	Sagittarius
♋	Cancer	♑	Capricorn
♌	Leo	♒	Aquarius
♍	Virgo	♓	Pisces

Planets

☉	Sun	♃	Jupiter
☽	Moon	♄	Saturn
☿	Mercury	♅	Uranus
♀	Venus	♆	Neptune
♂	Mars	♇	Pluto*

    While astrology has the power to alter and enhance one's life, the only catch is to learn the right way to do it. You now have all the knowledge you need to begin your spiritual exploration journey. If you have benefited from this knowledge, please share it around you with friends and relatives, helping your loved ones seek this positive path as well. Good luck! As established, this information can help you lead a happy life and get in touch with your true calling.

Here's another book by Silvia Hill that you might like

Free limited time bonus

Stop for a moment. I have a free bonus set up for you. The problem is that we forget 90% of everything that we read after 7 days. Crazy fact, right? Here's the solution: we've created a printable, 1-page pdf summary for this book that you're reading now. All you have to do to get your free pdf summary is to go to the following website: https://livetolearn.lpages.co/silviahill/
Once you do, it will be intuitive. Enjoy, and thank you!

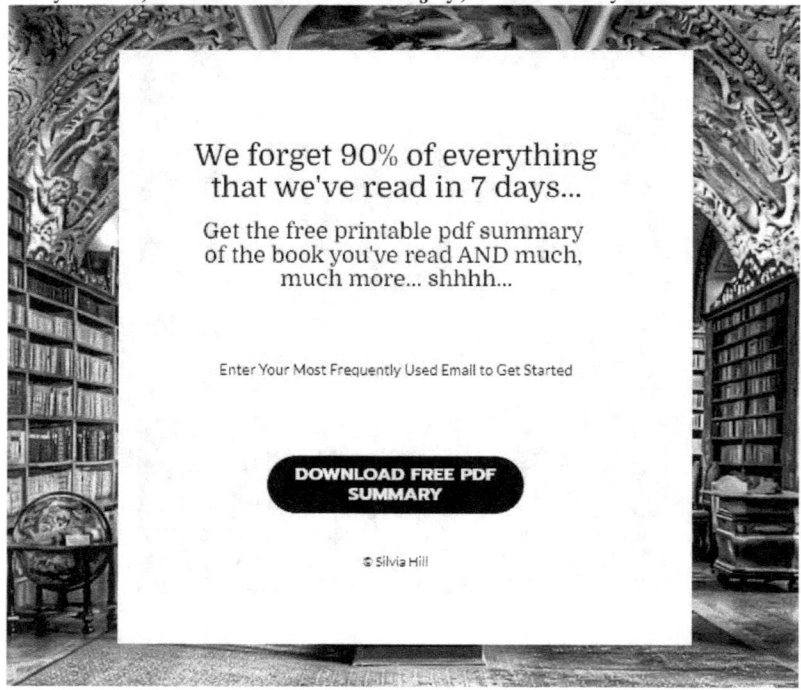

References

Campbell, C. (2014, August 16). A brief introduction to astrology. Retrieved from Com.au website: https://www.introinto.com.au/a-brief-introduction-to-astrology/

Groom, C. J. (n.d.). An introduction to astrology and zodiac signs. Retrieved from Westwoodhorizon.com website: https://westwoodhorizon.com/2018/10/an-introduction-to-astrology-and-zodiac-signs/

Hammonds, O. (2014, August 5). 3 benefits of astrology. Retrieved from 3Benefitsof.com website: https://www.3benefitsof.com/3-benefits-of-astrology/

Introductions to Astrology. (2020). In *Prognostication in the Medieval World* (pp. 814–817). De Gruyter.

Logan, J. (2017). *Astrology basics: A quick reference guide.* Jayne Logan.

As above, so below - astrology for Aquarius. (n.d.). Retrieved from Astrologyforaquarius.com website: https://astrologyforaquarius.com/articles/363/as-above-so-below/

Astrology planets and their meanings, planet symbols and cheat sheet. (2018, January 27). Retrieved from Labyrinthos.co website: https://labyrinthos.co/blogs/astrology-horoscope-zodiac-signs/astrology-planets-and-their-meanings-planet-symbols-and-cheat-sheet

AstroTwins. (2013, October 19). The 12 houses of the horoscope wheel. Retrieved from Astrostyle.com website: https://astrostyle.com/learn-astrology/the-12-zodiac-houses/

Kahn, N. (2020, July 29). The ruling planet for your zodiac sign & how it affects you. Retrieved from Bustle.com website: https://www.bustle.com/life/ruling-planet-zodiac-sign-meaning-astrology

Planets Signs & Houses - astrology information. (2013, January 4). Retrieved from Thejewelledsky.com website: https://thejewelledsky.com/articles/planets/

Team Jothishi. (2019, November 29). Classification of astrological knowledge - history, significance and more - jothishi. Retrieved from Jothishi.com website: https://jothishi.com/classification-of-astrological-knowledge-history-significance-and-more/

(N.d.). Retrieved from Costarastrology.com website: https://www.costarastrology.com/natal-chart/

12 astrology zodiac signs dates, meanings and compatibility. (n.d.). Retrieved from Astrology-zodiac-signs.com website: https://www.astrology-zodiac-signs.com/

FrancosWriter, E., & 04/02/, Z. (2021, April 2). Sun sign meaning: What the sun means for your zodiac sign. Retrieved from Yourtango.com website: https://www.yourtango.com/2019328837/what-your-sun-sign-means-astrology

Goodman, L. (2006). *Sun Signs*. Edinburgh, Scotland: George G. Harrap.

Hall, M. (n.d.). The Sun Sign. Retrieved from Liveabout.com website: https://www.liveabout.com/the-sun-sign-206735

Naylor, R. H. (2014). *Home astrology: A non-technical outline of popular astrology tradition*. Literary Licensing.

Rocks, D. (2019, September 25). What is A Sun Sign? Discover your purpose. Retrieved from Com.au website: https://www.starslikeyou.com.au/what-is-a-sun-sign/

Fenton, S. (1992). *Rising Signs*. London, England: Thorsons.

Maria. (2020, October 8). What is your Ascendant Sign & What does it Mean. Retrieved from Trusted-astrology.com website: https://trusted-astrology.com/how-does-your-ascendant-sign-affect-you/

Marie, A. (n.d.). Rising Sign - Ascendant. Retrieved from Astrosofa.com website: https://www.astrosofa.com/astrology/ascendant

Pemberton, B. (2021, May 6). What is my rising sign and what does it mean? *The Sun*. Retrieved from https://www.thesun.co.uk/fabulous/horoscopes/5621885/rising-sign-horoscope-calculate-meaning-star-sign-personality/

Sargent, C. (1990). *The astrology of rising signs*. London, England: Rider.

Secrets, M. A. (2019, October 4). Zodiac Text Symbols - not emoji - my astro secrets. Retrieved from Myastrosecrets.com website: https://myastrosecrets.com/zodiac-text-symbols-not-emoji/

Angel, J. (2015, April 6). *What's Your Emotional Mode of Operation?* Harper's BAZAAR. https://www.harpersbazaar.com/horoscopes/a10491/whats-your-emotional-mode-of-operation/

Balancing the Light and Dark: Understanding Your Sun and Moon in Astrology. (n.d.). Byrdie. https://www.byrdie.com/astrology-sun-and-moon-5086414

Cafe Astrology .com. (2021, March 14). *The Moon in Astrology/Zodiac.* https://cafeastrology.com/moon.html

Kahn, N. (2020, July 23). *How Each Planet's Astrology Directly Affects Every Zodiac Sign.* Bustle. https://www.bustle.com/life/how-each-planets-astrology-directly-affects-every-zodiac-sign-13098560

Moon Sign Calculator, Astrology Moon Phase Lunar Horoscope Online. (n.d.). Astro-Seek.Com. https://horoscopes.astro-seek.com/which-moon-phase-was-i-born-under-calculator

Contributor, G. (2020, November 23). *What is Numerology? How it can change your life?* The Times of India. https://timesofindia.indiatimes.com/astrology/numerology-tarot/what-is-numerology-how-it-can-change-your-life/articleshow/79314743.cms?from=mdr

Hurst, K. (2017, December 18). *Numerology: What is Numerology? And How Does it Work?* The Law Of Attraction. https://www.thelawofattraction.com/what-is-numerology/

J, S. (2021, March 30). *How Does Numerology Work with Astrology?* MIND IS THE MASTER. https://mindisthemaster.com/astrology-and-numerology/

Numerology: History, Origins, & More - Astrology.com. (n.d.). Astrology. https://www.astrology.com/numerology

Numerology number characteristics. Learn what your numbers mean. (n.d.). See You. Be You. https://seeyoubeyou.com/pages/numbers

Destiny Numbers. (n.d.). Retrieved from Prokerala.com website: https://www.prokerala.com/numerology/destiny-numbers.htm

Felicia. (2017, March 23). What your Destiny number reveals about your life purpose. Retrieved from Feliciabender.com website: https://feliciabender.com/the-destiny-or-expression-number/

GOSTICA. (2017, March 23). THIS is what your Destiny Number is saying about your life. Retrieved from Gostica.com website: https://gostica.com/spiritual-lifestyle/destiny-number-saying-life/

McClain, M. (n.d.). Numerology - the birth name. Retrieved from Astrology-numerology.com website: http://astrology-numerology.com/num-birthname.html

Coughlin, S. (2021, January 19). Your life path number is more than A personality type. Retrieved from Refinery29.com website: https://www.refinery29.com/en-us/life-path-number-numerology-meaning

Faragher, A. K. (2020, April 10). Numerology 101: How to calculate life path & Destiny numbers. Retrieved from Allure website: https://www.allure.com/story/numerology-how-to-calculate-life-path-destiny-number

Hurst, K. (2015, December 15). Numerology calculator: Your life path number and meaning. Retrieved from Thelawofattraction.com website: https://www.thelawofattraction.com/life-path-number-challenges/

the Cut. (2020, May 14). What is your life-path number? Retrieved from Thecut.com website: https://www.thecut.com/article/life-path-number.html

Adams, A. (n.d.). *Personality Number – what others see when they first meet you*. Retrieved from https://thesagedivine.com/personality-number/

Decoz, H., & World Numerology. (2001, September 1). Do Your Own Numerology Reading - Personality. Retrieved from Worldnumerology.com website: https://www.worldnumerology.com/Do-reading-numerology-02-Personality.html

Discover your personality number / numerology calculator. (n.d.). Retrieved from https://mattbeech.com/numerology/personality-number/

Adams, A. (n.d.). *Heart's Desire / Soul Urge number / meanings, calculations, and more*. Retrieved from https://thesagedivine.com/hearts-desire-number/

Heart's Desire number - numerology center. (n.d.). Retrieved from Numerology.center website: http://numerology.center/heart_desire.php

The Heart's Desire Number. (2009, July 30). Retrieved from Tsemrinpoche.com website: https://www.tsemrinpoche.com/tsem-tulku-rinpoche/numerology/the-hearts-desire-number.html

A brief history of tarot cards – articles. (n.d.). Retrieved from Bicyclecards.com website: https://bicyclecards.com/article/a-brief-history-of-tarot-cards/

Brigit. (2018, May 9). What are Tarot cards + how do they work? Retrieved from Biddytarot.com website: https://www.biddytarot.com/what-is-tarot-how-does-it-work/

Tarot card meanings. (2011a, December 15). Retrieved from Biddytarot.com website: https://www.biddytarot.com/tarot-card-meanings/major-arcana/

Tarot card meanings. (2011b, December 18). Retrieved from Biddytarot.com website: https://www.biddytarot.com/tarot-card-meanings/minor-arcana/

Tarot.com Staff. (2019, February 25). The Major Arcana Tarot card meanings. Retrieved from Tarot.com website: https://www.tarot.com/tarot/cards/major-arcana

(N.d.). Retrieved from Squarespace.com website: https://static1.squarespace.com/static/5a07aca112abd96680bdc6fa/t/5b1d983d8a922ddcbe3a0ac4/1528666185262/MAJOR+%26+MINOR+ARCANA+QUICK+REFERENCE+SHEET.pdf

Coryna, O. (2020, November 22). Sagittarius energy & the Temperance card. Retrieved from Lilithastrology.com

Faragher, A. K. (2021, April 28). The personality of an Aries, explained. Retrieved from Allure website: https://www.allure.com/story/aries-zodiac-sign-personality-traits

King of wands tarot card meanings - aquarian insight. (2013, December 1). Retrieved from Aquarianinsight.com website: https://www.aquarianinsight.com/tarot-card-meanings/minor-arcana/suit-of-wands/king-of-wands/

Philips, S. (2019, April 28). Tarot cards for each zodiac sign. Retrieved from Tarot.com website: https://www.tarot.com/astrology/tarot-cards

SawyerAuthor, A., & 12/28/, Z. (2018, December 28). What tarot cards represent each of the zodiac signs in astrology. Retrieved from Yourtango.com website: https://www.yourtango.com/2018317524/how-tarot-cards-and-astrology-zodiac-signs-are-connected

Steve. (2019, December 4). What tarot card represents Leo? Retrieved from Vekkesind.com website: https://vekkesind.com/what-tarot-card-represents-leo/

Steve. (2020, January 28). What Tarot card is associated with Aries? Retrieved from Vekkesind.com website: https://vekkesind.com/what-tarot-card-is-associated-with-aries/

Tarot card meanings. (2011, December 15). Retrieved from Biddytarot.com website: https://www.biddytarot.com/tarot-card-meanings/minor-arcana/suit-of-wands/

Tarot.com Staff. (2016, July 14). A taste of tarot: Strength & Leo. Retrieved from Tarot.com website: https://www.tarot.com/tarot/strength-tarot-card-leo-zodiac-sign

Earth signs will inspire you with their groundedness. (2020, August 12). Retrieved from Cosmopolitan.com website: https://www.cosmopolitan.com/lifestyle/a33588028/earth-signs-astrology/

Knight of Pentacles: Upright and reversed love meanings & more. (n.d.). Retrieved from Kasamba.com website: https://www.kasamba.com/tarot-reading/decks/minor-arcana/knight-of-pentacles-card/

Page of Pentacles: Upright and reversed love meanings & more. (n.d.). Retrieved from Kasamba.com website: https://www.kasamba.com/tarot-reading/decks/minor-arcana/page-of-pentacles-card/

PSA: Your zodiac sign has its own tarot card. (2020, March 25). Retrieved from Cosmopolitan.com website: https://www.cosmopolitan.com/lifestyle/a31913908/tarot-cards-zodiac-signs-astrology/

Slozberg, M. (2020, April 4). 10 tarot cards that represent earth signs. Retrieved from Thetalko.com website: https://www.thetalko.com/tarot-cards-that-represent-earth-signs/

Virgo through the eyes of tarot. (2016, October 15). Retrieved from Tarotelements.com website: https://tarotelements.com/virgo-through-the-eyes-of-tarot/

Air signs can talk, think, and network faster than the wind. (2020, July 14). Retrieved from Cosmopolitan.com website: https://www.cosmopolitan.com/lifestyle/a33314375/air-signs-astrology/

Cabral, C. (n.d.). The 10 fundamental Libra traits and the best advice for Libras. Retrieved from Prepscholar.com website: https://blog.prepscholar.com/libra-traits-personality

Mukomolova, G. (2018, September 28). What tarot cards correspond to your zodiac signs. Retrieved from Nylon.com website: https://www.nylon.com/articles/what-tarot-cards-zodiac-signs

Steve. (2019, December 17). What tarot card represents Gemini? Retrieved from Vekkesind.com website: https://vekkesind.com/what-tarot-card-represents-gemini/

Tarot.com Staff. (2018a, January 15). A taste of tarot: Aquarius and The Star. Retrieved from Tarot.com website: https://www.tarot.com/tarot/star-tarot-card-aquarius-zodiac-sign

Tarot.com Staff. (2018b, September 25). A taste of tarot: Justice & Libra. Retrieved from Tarot.com website: https://www.tarot.com/tarot/justice-tarot-card-libra-zodiac-sign

The tarot suit of Swords meanings & interpretation. (2014, April 3). Retrieved from Sunsigns.org website: https://www.sunsigns.org/tarot-suit-of-swords-minor-arcana/

(N.d.). Retrieved from Gyanswers.com

Cabral, C. (n.d.). The 10 Scorpio personality traits to know. Retrieved from Prepscholar.com website: https://blog.prepscholar.com/scorpio-personality-traits

Carrillo, G. J. R. (2017). A King of Cups. In A. M. G. López & A. Farnsworth-Alvear (Trans.), *The Colombia Reader* (pp. 113–117). Duke University Press.

DLC Tarot Notebooks. (2019). *Page of cups: Tarot diary log book, record and interpret readings, lined notebook journal for tarot lovers.* Independently Published.

Douglas, M. (n.d.). The fundamental 6 Pisces traits, explained. Retrieved from Prepscholar.com website: https://blog.prepscholar.com/pisces-traits

Knight of Wands Tarot card meanings. (2011, December 22). Retrieved from Biddytarot.com website: https://www.biddytarot.com/tarot-card-meanings/minor-arcana/suit-of-wands/knight-of-wands/

Mantis Tarot. (2020, September 4). The chariot & cancer: The power of moving waters. Retrieved from Mantistarot.com website: https://mantistarot.com/2020/09/03/the-chariot-cancer-the-power-of-moving-waters/

Tarot card meanings. (2011, December 15). Retrieved from Biddytarot.com website: https://www.biddytarot.com/tarot-card-meanings/minor-arcana/suit-of-cups/

Tarot.com Staff. (2016, February 17). A taste of tarot: Pisces and The Moon. Retrieved from Tarot.com website: https://www.tarot.com/tarot/moon-tarot-card-pisces-zodiac-sign

Wen, B. (2019, October 29). Tarot's death card & the season of Scorpio - north Atlantic books. Retrieved from Northatlanticbooks.com website: https://www.northatlanticbooks.com/blog/tarots-death-card-the-season-of-scorpio/

(N.d.). Retrieved from Costarastrology.com website: https://www.costarastrology.com/zodiac-signs/cancer-sign

Brigit. (2016, January 13). Tarot by numbers: A fast and simple way to learn the cards with numerology. Retrieved from Biddytarot.com website: https://www.biddytarot.com/tarot-by-numbers/

Numerology of Tarot. (n.d.). Retrieved from Thethreadsoffate.com website: https://www.thethreadsoffate.com/blogs/news/numerology-of-tarot

Tarot & numerology - minor Arcana ace to ten - tarot study. (2015, July 1). Retrieved from Tarot-study.info website: https://tarot-study.info/articles/tarot-numerology-minor-arcana-ace-to-ten/

Tarot and Numerology: What do numbers in Tarot Mean for the Minor Arcana? (Infographic). (2016, November 14). Retrieved from Labyrinthos.co website:

https://labyrinthos.co/blogs/learn-tarot-with-labyrinthos-academy/tarot-and-numerology-what-do-numbers-in-tarot-mean-for-the-minor-arcana-infographic

Tarot.com Staff. (2019, May 2). The Minor Arcana: Meanings behind the number cards. Retrieved from Tarot.com website: https://www.tarot.com/tarot/meaning-of-numbers-in-minor-arcana

The minor Arcana: How numbers and elements give tarot meaning. (n.d.). Retrieved from Gaia.com website: https://www.gaia.com/article/the-minor-arcana-how-numbers-and-elements-give-tarot-meaning

The Numerologist Team. (2010, February 13). Numerology and the minor Arcana cards in Tarot - numerologist.Com. Retrieved from Numerologist.com website: https://numerologist.com/numerology/numerology-and-the-tarot/

Chris, & Styles, S. (2020, June 12). Numerology meanings of Tarot Major Arcana. Retrieved from 365Pincode.com website: https://365pincode.com/numerology-meanings-of-tarot-major-arcana/

Major Arcana Correspondences. (2018, August 17). Retrieved from Tarotelements.com website: https://tarotelements.com/major-arcana-correspondences/

Meg. (2010, March 25). Numerological & astrological attributes of the Major Arcana. Retrieved from Padmes.com website: https://padmes.com/2010/03/numerological-astrolgical-attributes-of-the-major-arcana/

This story behind the Tarot major Arcana mirrors human experience. (n.d.). Retrieved from Gaia.com website: https://www.gaia.com/article/journey-of-the-tarot-how-major-arcana-meanings-mirror-the-soul

Boswell, L. (2017, August 28). Planet correspondences in astrology and Tarot — Lisa Boswell. Retrieved from Divinationandfortunetelling.com website: https://divinationandfortunetelling.com/articles/2017/8/28/planet-correspondences-in-astrology-tarot-and-divination

Mantis Tarot. (2020, April 20). The astrology of the Major Arcana: The planets. Retrieved from Mantistarot.com website: https://mantistarot.com/2020/04/20/the-astrology-of-the-major-arcana-the-planets/

Media, H. (n.d.). The tarot & planetary correspondences. Retrieved from Voxxthepsychic.com website: https://voxxthepsychic.com/tarotplanets.html

12 Houses Zodiac Tarot spread. (2015, December 21). Retrieved from Angelorum.co website: https://angelorum.co/topics/divination/12-houses-zodiac-tarot-spread/

learntarot. (2018, November 27). Learning & using the Zodiac Tarot Spread. Retrieved from Thesimpletarot.com website: https://thesimpletarot.com/learning-using-zodiac-tarot-spread/

Waits, P. (2020, July 23). Tarot spreads: The 3 most effective card spreads. Retrieved from themagichoroscope.com website: https://themagichoroscope.com/zodiac/tarot-spreads

Wigington, P. (n.d.). How to use the Celtic Cross spread in Tarot. Retrieved from Learnreligions.com website: https://www.learnreligions.com/the-celtic-cross-spread-2562796

Regan, S. (2021, January 21). The simplest tarot "spread" for quick insight anytime you need it. Retrieved from Mindbodygreen.com website: https://www.mindbodygreen.com/articles/one-card-tarot

Crawford, C. (2019, December 21). How to use a 3 card tarot spread for self care — the self-care emporium. Retrieved from Theselfcareemporium.com website: https://theselfcareemporium.com/blog/tarot-card-spread-self-care

Astrology symbols and glyphs. (2015, April 16). Retrieved from Cafeastrology.com website: https://cafeastrology.com/astrology-symbols-glyphs.html